Crab De

of the Chesapeake Bay

⊹Virginia Edition⊹

www.crabdecksandtikibars.com

By Susan Elnicki Wade and Bill Wade

This book is dedicated to Max and Nicholas,

who picked crabs and kept us happy
while we wrote our second book

ISBN: 978-1-4781-8892-6

Authors: Susan Elnicki Wade and Bill Wade
Photographs by Susan Elnicki Wade
Maps by Bill Wade
Illustrations by Samantha Simon

Printed in the United States of America

For additional copies of this book visit **www.crabdecksandtikibars.com**

Or contact us at
2916 Northampton Street, NW
Washington, DC 20015
(202) 531-7135
susan@crabdecksandtikibars.com
bill@crabdecksandtikibars.com

Table of Contents

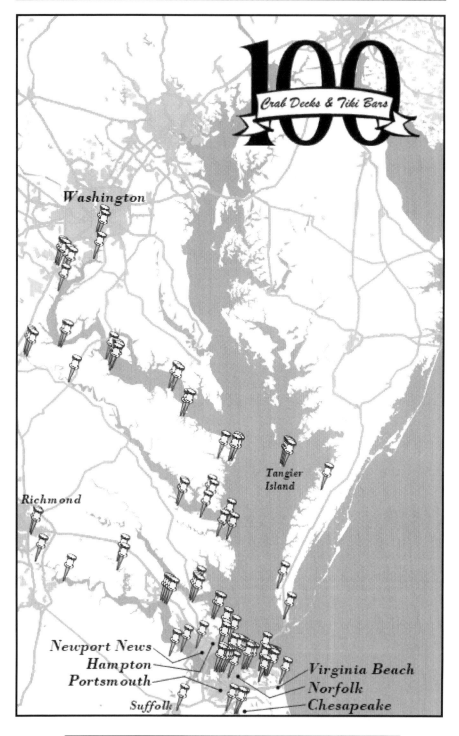

Crab Decks & Tiki Bars of the Chesapeake Bay, Virginia Edition

Introduction

The day I saw a man dressed in colonial attire drinking a beer in front of a palm tree with tiki lights, I knew we were in for a unique adventure.

A few months earlier, we'd launched our first travel guide, *Crab Decks & Tiki Bars of the Chesapeake Bay*, and thought we'd give ourselves time to recover from months of dashing around the Bay, investigating waterfront eateries, and sampling the wares at every port.

Unfortunately, taking a break from travel writing was not in the cards. Our first book covered Maryland extensively, but we ran out of steam before researching Virginia eateries. We thought that an appendix would satisfy crab and tiki fans in the Old Dominion. Instead, scores of e-mails poured in from the Bay's southern waters, asking for their fair share.

It seemed like a reasonable request, but we wondered if we could afford the time and expense of writing another book. Part of us missed the excitement of discovering new seafood places and exploring remote necks of the Bay. And we felt compelled to complete our task and cover every inch of Chesapeake coastline.

After many late-night debates, writing a second book seemed like a good idea, so we decided to break the news to our sons. At first it was fun, but they'd been dragged along on so many research trips that they grew weary of their parents' project. One son still amiably picks crabs with his dad but keeps an eye on the clock for when he can return to friends and video games. Our other boy defiantly orders cheeseburgers and throws French fries at seagulls. It was a tough sell, but we got eventually got our entire family on board and began venturing out to Virginia's Chesapeake Bay.

Travel logistics presented challenges with time and distance. We could drive to Annapolis and back in a day before the boys got out of school. But outside of Northern Virginia, most locations entailed a three-hour drive, so we planned more extensive trips. Our 20-year anniversary, my birthday, and spring break turned into major crab deck excursions.

Our sacrifices yielded delightful rewards, because Virginians are passionate about their seafood. We saw rusty crab pots piled high at marinas and witnessed the revival of Chesapeake oysters at aquafarms on the Rappahannock. Shrimp came with grits, and the aroma of Old Bay and steamed crabs filled the air. Southern sides like fried green tomatoes, okra, and hush puppies added a lovely twist to our plates. Newly enamored with Virginia's spin on Bay cuisine, I served York River oyster stuffing with my Christmas turkey.

Places we'd never seen before somehow felt familiar. Virginia's Eastern Shore was home to the same beautiful marshlands that we'd found on Hooper Island. Norfolk's bustling port and urban skyline rivaled Baltimore's Inner Harbor. A tiki bar at Colonial Beach planted palm trees as tall as the ones on Solomons Island. On rustic crab deck tables, wooden mallets and brown paper were required and regional differences were washed away by the Bay's waters.

We hope you enjoy our second book and feel inspired to explore the wonderful waters of the Chesapeake Bay. To see photos or read the blog from our Virginia adventures, visit us on Facebook or go to **www.crabdecksandtikibars.com**

— Susan Elnicki Wade

About the Book

Crab Decks & Tiki Bars of the Chesapeake Bay, Virginia Edition is the second in a series of destination guides to authentic seafood restaurants, crab shacks, and tiki bars on the Bay. Eateries chosen for this book must be located on the Chesapeake Bay or its tributary rivers and creeks. We believe if you can't see the water, you don't get the full Bay experience. Restaurants must also serve local crabs to make the cut for the book.

The book is divided into seven regions. Each entry starts with contact info (address, phone, and web site), followed by:
- County in Virginia where it's located,
- When It's Open (year-round or seasonal),
- Latitude and Longitude,
- Body of Water,
- Dockage, and
- Distance from major cities.

Every crab deck and tiki bar profile includes a map and photograph taken on-site. Our one-of-a-kind Atmosphere Meter rates the ambience, ranging from casual to formal on a scale of one to 10 (frosty beer mugs to crisp martinis).

Crab Decks & Tiki Bars of the Chesapeake Bay, Virginia Edition provides in-depth descriptions that paint a vivid image of each restaurant's décor, atmosphere, cuisine, specialties, and surroundings, letting you know what to expect when you arrive. Many profiles include a bonus: colorful history, folklore, culture, and traditions unique to each neck of the Bay.

At the back of the book, three indexes are provided to help locate the seafood houses you want to visit: Body of Water, City and Restaurant Name. The handy Tiki Tracker encourages you to document your own Bay adventures.

About the Authors

Bill Wade was born and raised in Maryland. His father, a former DC fire fighter, hadn't intended to become a waterman — until Bill's mom entered a jingle-writing contest for a local car dealership and won a boat. Their wooden cabin cruiser, *Limey*, was built on the Chesapeake Bay and docked at Kent Narrows. Summers were spent cruising around the remote necks of the Bay and catching crabs with chicken necks tied to the end of strings. Bill can pick a crab faster than most workers at a Phillips processing plant.

Susan Elnicki Wade grew up in Oil City, a small blue-collar town in western Pennsylvania, eating native brook trout that she and her brothers caught from Allegheny mountain streams. The closest she'd come in her youth to a blue crab were the crawfish they used as bait. She worked in restaurants in Pittsburgh, New York, and Washington, DC. Picking crabs still doesn't come easy to her, even after visiting every county along the Bay over the past two decades. But she can whip up a mean batch of fried oysters and recently baked her first Smith Island Cake.

Bill and Susan live in Washington, DC, with their two sons. The Wades each have 20+ years experience in the publishing industry and hope to make enough money on this book to buy a boat. Their first travel guide, *Crab Decks & Tiki Bars of the Chesapeake Bay*, sold to thousands of readers across the mid-Atlantic. To contact the authors or learn about the books, find them on Facebook or go to **www.crabdecksandtikibars.com**

About the Web Site

Now that you have a copy of *Crab Decks & Tiki Bars of the Chesapeake Bay, Virginia Edition*, please visit the companion web site, **www.crabdecksandtikibars.com.** We added new features to make the book more useful and your Bay excursions more enjoyable.

- **Crab Deck Updates** report on Chesapeake seafood houses that just opened or closed their doors after the book when to press.

- **Captain's Blog** chronicles our adventures as we continue to cruise the Bay investigating new crab decks and tiki bars.

- **Photo Gallery** of all the restaurants in the book to give you a clear picture of where you're headed.

 # Bay Travel Tips

At times during our trips around the Bay, we felt like seasoned explorers, successfully navigating Virginia's back roads and hidden creeks without a hitch. Other times, we made mistakes that took a little wind out of our sails. To make your trips run smoothly:

- **Call first.** Most destinations are family-run businesses that can have irregular hours, especially in the off-season. Give them a ring to see if they're open when you plan to arrive.

- **Use every navigation tool.** Grab a map, your GPS, nautical charts, and charge up your smart phone. Many crab decks are located off the beaten path where roads are poorly marked.

- **Plan ahead but be flexible.** The unexpected is bound to happen – like waiting for boats to pass under a drawbridge or getting stuck on a road behind a dilapidated chicken truck. That's the Bay's charm, and it adds color to your travel tales.

- **Eat food in season.** Chesapeake aficionados say you should only eat oysters in months with an "r," and crabs bought off-season are rarely local. So ask your server what's fresh, even if you had your heart set on something else. Every season on the Bay offers unique delicacies that are worth the wait.

Crab Decks & Tiki Bars
of the Chesapeake Bay

⁎Virginia Edition⁎

www.crabdecksandtikibars.com

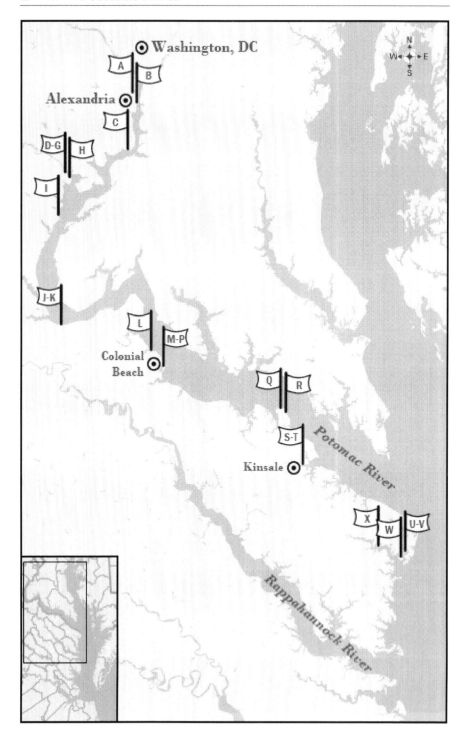

Potomac River

Indigo Landing Restaurant

1 Marina Drive
Alexandria, VA 22314
703-548-0001
www.indigolanding.com

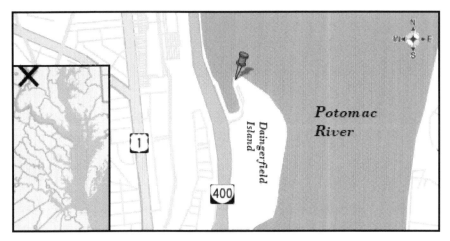

County: Alexandria (city)
Open: Year Round
Latitude: N 38° 49' 59" ⚓ Longitude: W 77° 2' 31"
Body of Water: Potomac River
Dockage: Yes
Driving Distance: Richmond: 106 miles,
Norfolk: 191 miles, Washington, DC: 6 miles

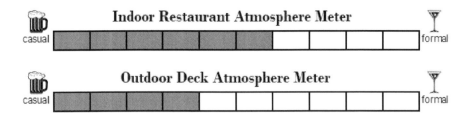

Most waterfront eateries offer views of boats and ducks, but Indigo Landing's got something special — airplanes. Just one mile south of Reagan National Airport, you can relax on the large deck and gaze at planes ascending into the sky. In the distance, you can see the Washington skyline, monuments, and capitol dome. Night or day, it's fabulous.

The restaurant is next to Washington Sailing Marina on Daingerfield Island, which isn't really an island, but a wooded park surrounded on most sides by the Potomac River. It was established in 1696 as part of Alexandria, but most of the settlers here were killed by Indians, diphtheria, or malaria.

Today's visitors fare much better at this lovely setting. The décor is tastefully contemporary. A fireplace warms the lounge, and subtle nautical artwork brightens the walls. The menu presents casual dishes, such as pulled pork, steamed mussels, and lamb burgers.

Dinner highpoints include crab cakes, pan-roasted salmon, crispy rock shrimp, and steak. At Sunday brunch, you can choose among stations for seafood, beef, ham, omelets, or waffles. And when you toast the incredible view, consult the libation menu's specialty cocktails like Old Salty Dog, Island Breeze, or Joyful Almond.

Chart House Restaurant

1 Cameron Street
Alexandria, VA 22314
703-685-5080
www.chart-house.com

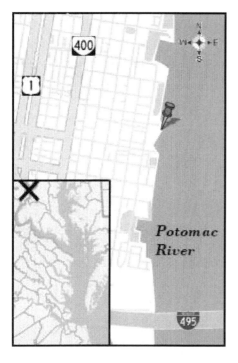

County: Alexandria (city)

Open: Year Round

Latitude: N 38° 48' 19"

Longitude: W 77° 2' 19"

Body of Water: Potomac River

Dockage: No

Driving Distance:
  Richmond: 104 miles
  Norfolk: 190 miles
  Washington, DC: 8 miles

 Atmosphere Meter

casual | | | | | | | | | | | formal

The pulse of Old Town Alexandria's waterfront beats at Chart House. From its deck, you can watch people water taxi to National Harbor, climb aboard the Peach Blossom paddle wheel boat, or attend exhibits at Torpedo Factory Art Center. The restaurant's plain turquoise exterior understates the interior's vibrant contemporary décor, which highlights the blues, greens, and gold of water. Colorful artwork around the walls and streams of glass bubbles dangling from chandeliers provide a whimsical visual display in the dining rooms.

This expansive place is a seafood lover's paradise. Raw bar favorites include just-shucked oysters and tuna tartare. Rockfish, crab cakes, and flounder represent the local catch, and imports like grilled salmon, lobster rolls, and Alaskan king crab legs are welcome additions. Fresh greens and vegetables create a tempting salad bar, and meat eaters can get their fill of steak, chicken, or prime rib. The Hot Chocolate Lava Cake with molten center redefines decadence in signature desserts.

If good food at an attractive restaurant isn't enough, then go out and explore the attractions in Old Town. Founded in 1749, it hosts 20+ historic sites from colonial times to the Civil War. Antique shops, chic boutiques, art galleries, museums, lively pubs, and 18th century row houses line the cobblestone streets. Early American heritage mixed with modern flair make Alexandria an ideal destination.

Cedar Knoll Restaurant

9030 Lucia Lane
Alexandria, VA 22308
703-799-1501
www.cedarknollinnrestaurant.com

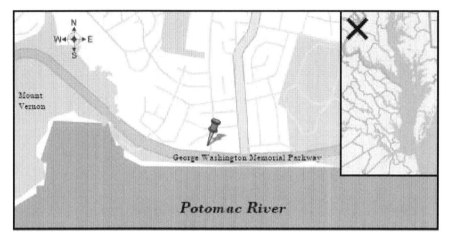

County: Alexandria (city)
Open: Year Round
Latitude: N 38° 42' 38" ⚓ Longitude: W 77° 3' 56"
Body of Water: Potomac River
Dockage: No
Driving Distance: Richmond: 99 miles,
Norfolk: 184 miles, Washington, DC: 15 miles

Atmosphere Meter

casual 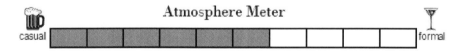 formal

Cedar Knoll is the place to come and be part of history. Ownership of the property dates back to the days of George Washington. The building was constructed in the 1800s as a tenant farmhouse for the Markland Plantation. In 1909, the owner, Dr. Bliss, lost the property in a poker game. During

World War I, it was used as a convalescent hospital for soldiers returning home from the front. Fort Belvoir is just a short drive away, and Mount Vernon, the birthplace of our nation's first president, is the must-see attraction in the area.

The location is splendid, with a spectacular view of boats drifting down the Potomac and bicyclists riding on the trails. The inside of the restaurant has an old-fashioned feel. Floral print overlays cover white linen tablecloths, and a pair of gorgeous fireplaces warms the air in winter. But on a sunny summer day, the best seats in the house are on the outdoor patio where the atmosphere is casual and carefree.

The menu quenches the thirst of tourists from nearby historic sites, as well as diners looking for a romantic setting. You can nibble on fried calamari, baked brie, or hummus with pita after a long hike along the river. Empanadas, burgers, and sandwiches come with fries.

Signature dishes: Spanish paella simmered with seafood, chorizo, and chicken, and roast duck sweetened with cognac and grilled fruit. Pasta plays a major role among the entrees, and seafood specialties include pecan-crusted salmon, rainbow trout, and shrimp in a spicy marinara sauce. The Executive Supreme steak is a ravenous carnivore's dream.

Occoquan Inn
Restaurant & Tavern

301 Mill Street
Occoquan, VA 22125
703-491-1888
www.occoquaninn.com

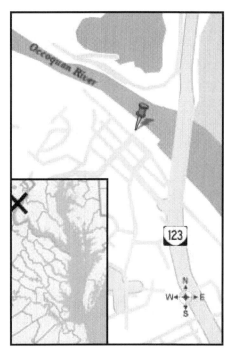

County: Prince William
  County

Open: Year Round

Latitude: N 38° 41' 2"

Longitude: W 77° 15' 36"

Body of Water: Occoquan
  River off the Potomac River

Dockage: No

Driving Distance:
  Richmond: 88 miles
  Norfolk: 173 miles
  Washington, DC: 23 miles

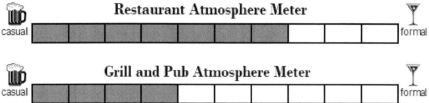

Occoquan Inn is full of delightful surprises. This
charming historic building has three dining areas, each with

distinct personalities, and on top of that — a ghost! The story of the house spirit dates back to the early 1800s when the inn was built.

According to local lore, an amorous Indian was spending time with the innkeeper's wife. One night, the husband caught the Indian coming down the wooden stairs and shot him dead before he reached the last step. Since that fateful day, the Indian's regal face and long black hair have appeared in the upstairs ladies room mirror.

The inn's main section offers upscale dining in a warm atmosphere accented by antique stained glass and vintage photos of American heroes. It's ideal for romantic dates or special events. Seafood ranges from local crab cakes and rockfish to broiled scallops and salmon. You can choose from a variety of steaks, including the stand-out Beef Jefferson that has twin filets on pastry shells in a wild mushroom sauce.

Virginia Grill serves more casual fare indoors or out on the deck overlooking the river. Sandwiches and burgers come with chips. The kitchen shows its Southern roots with dishes such as Virginia peanut soup, Confederate chili topped with cheddar cheese and onions, chicken and biscuits, and home-style meatloaf with mashed potatoes.

Down Under Pub features live music, electronic dartboards, several TVs, and a limited menu for nibbling.

Madigan's Waterfront Restaurant

201 Mill Street
Occoquan, VA 22125
703-494-6373
www.madiganswaterfront.com

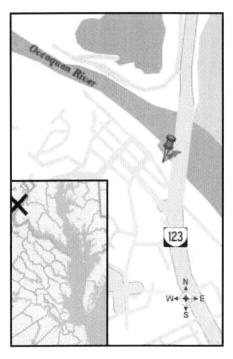

County: Prince William
  County

Open: Year Round

Latitude: N 38° 40' 59"

Longitude: W 77° 15' 32"

Body of Water: Occoquan
  River off the Potomac River

Dockage: Yes

Driving Distance:
  Richmond: 88 miles
  Norfolk: 173 miles
  Washington, DC: 23 miles

Atmosphere Meter

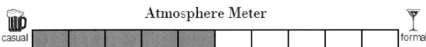

casual ▓▓▓▓▓░░░░░ formal

Crabs and history collide at Madigan's Waterfront Restaurant. It's located in a big old building, rich in vintage charm with exposed brick walls and thick wooden beams holding up the ceiling. Hanging planters with streams of ivy dangle over cozy booths in the dining room. In the bar, you'll find a row of dartboards and a stage for bands. The upstairs

banquet room is a popular venue for special events. The outdoor deck and tiki bar offer a terrific vantage point to watch the stars come out over the Occoquan River.

Madigan's extensive menu specializes in seafood, yet covers all the bases. Breakfast plates get your day going with three-egg omelets, waffles, and sausage gravy with biscuits. The appetizer menu presents tasty variations on crab, shrimp, and oysters, as well as snacks like cheese plates and hummus. Entrees continue the seafood theme with plump crab cakes, stuffed shrimp, and pecan-crusted flounder. Several cuts of steak, chicken alfredo, and oversized sandwiches play to every diner's whim. Try to leave room in your belly for decadent desserts like Reeses Pie and Madigan's Mountain of chocolate cake topped with ice cream and Oreo crumbs.

After you finish your feast, you might need to burn off some calories, so take a walk around historic Occoquan. In colonial times, the town bustled with a grist mill, tobacco warehouse, and ships transporting wood, fish, and river ice. During the Civil War, it served as a postal hub for the North and the South. Today, Occoquan's antique shops, galleries, and historic buildings make it an ideal day-trip location.

The Electric Palm Restaurant

12745 Sea Ray Lane
Woodbridge, VA 22192
703-492-7256
www.theelectricpalm.net

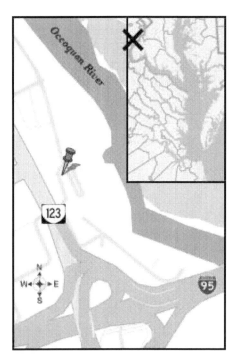

County: Prince William
  County

Open: Year Round

Latitude: N 38° 40' 31"

Longitude: W 77° 15' 14"

Body of Water: Occoquan
  River off the Potomac River

Dockage: Yes

Driving Distance:
  Richmond: 87 miles
  Norfolk: 172 miles
  Washington, DC: 22 miles

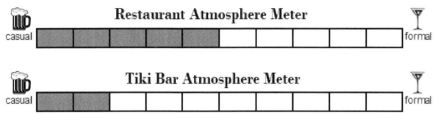

When you pull into The Electric Palm you get two restaurant experiences for the price of one. The upstairs dining room is showered in light through tall windows that stretch up to the ceiling. It's open and airy, yet still cozy. White tablecloths and a black baby grand piano in the corner suggest you might want to put on a clean shirt before sitting down to dinner. Doors open onto a long patio that overlooks Prince William Marina.

The ambience switches to casual when you head downstairs to the energetic tiki bar. Its thatched roof, Polynesian masks, and hanging surfboards tempt you to slide onto a wooden bar stool and order a mai-tai. An electric red palm tree casts a rosy glow on the deck outside.

Food is hearty, well-cooked, and combines fresh seafood with American cuisine. Maryland-style crab cakes, blackened mahi-mahi with shrimp, and baby back ribs steal the show.

Best of all, the location offers options for any mood. You can hang out and watch the boats cruise into the marina, or take a leisurely stroll into downtown Occoquan to check out the historic buildings, antique stores, and gift shops.

Water's Edge Seafood & Steaks

13188 Marina Way
Woodbridge, VA 22192
703-494-5000
www.watersedgeoccoquan.com

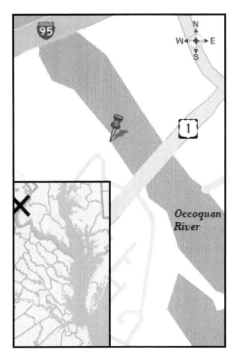

County: Prince William
  County

Open: Year Round

Latitude: N 38° 40' 8"

Longitude: W 77° 14' 35"

Body of Water: Occoquan
  River off the Potomac River

Dockage: Yes

Driving Distance:
  Richmond: 87 miles
  Norfolk: 173 miles
  Washington, DC: 22 miles

Atmosphere Meter

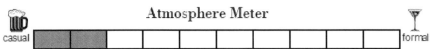

casual ⬛⬛☐☐☐☐☐☐☐☐ formal

Water's Edge already had the biggest outdoor deck in the metro area, but that wasn't enough. They added a new upper deck with a second tiki bar to make room for everyone who wants to kick back, watch bands, and grab a bite to eat. From the parking lot Water's Edge looks like a standard seafood restaurant, but guests arriving by water are overwhelmed with the size of this building and the buzz of activity inside.

For entertainment you can enjoy live bands on weekends, country tunes on Thursday, karaoke on Tuesday, summer bikini contests, half-price appetizers during football games, poker runs for charity, and beer pong tournaments. The 20 flat-screen TVs give sports fans something to cheer about.

A recently updated menu aims to please every dining preference. Appetizers help get your seafood groove going with crab dip, fried calamari, steamed shrimp, and tuna bites. Wings, mozzarella sticks, and nachos add to the snack list. Sandwiches accommodate meat-lovers' whims with Cuban roast pork, steak and cheese, reubens, and chicken wraps.

Your mouth will water when they pull ribs, beef brisket, and pork from the smoker. And if you're in the mood to pick crabs, you can order them by the dozen or tackle an all-you-can-eat feast.

If you feel lucky, head over to the Lobster Zone near the front door where you can lower a big claw into a live lobster tank and try to catch your dinner. Why not? At Water's Edge, it's all about having a good time.

Osprey's Landing Restaurant

401 Belmont Bay Drive
Woodbridge, VA 22191
703-494-1935
www.ospreysgolf.com/woodbridge-dining

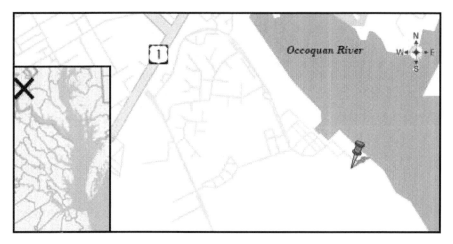

County: Prince William County
Open: Year Round
Latitude: N 38° 39' 8" ⚓ Longitude: W 77° 13' 49"
Body of Water: Belmont Bay off the Potomac River
Dockage: Yes
Driving Distance: Richmond: 89 miles,
Norfolk: 174 miles, Washington, DC: 24 miles

Atmosphere Meter

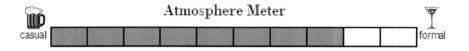

casual · formal

If golf is your game, then you'll score a birdie at Osprey's Landing. It's got fresh local seafood plus an award-winning course — all in one location. Open to the public, the restaurant serves as the 19th hole for a course designed by

Preston Caruthers and Bob Mortensen and is rated among the "Top 100 Must-Play" mid-Atlantic courses.

The front brick patio is set back from the water, with a sweeping lawn, old oak trees, and grazing geese between you and the river. The back deck overlooks a well-groomed putting green, and townhouses stand in a row next door.

It's no surprise that local brides choose this place for their big day. Recent renovations have created an elegant, country venue with 14-foot vaulted ceilings, graceful chandeliers, and soft green walls that accent the rich dark woodwork and floor. Naturalist waterfowl artwork hangs over cushioned booths.

The chef's classic American cuisine captures the best of the season's harvest. Calamari arrives with fresh lemon aioli, and crispy pork belly is lacquered with blackberry molasses. Salads are tossed with local spring greens, and sandwiches range from honey-smoked salmon to juicy Angus burgers. Irresistible entrees include fish and chips in a Sam Adams beer batter, scallops with pumpkin risotto, and roasted rockfish with turnip puree. Ice cream made in-house is the perfect partner for chocolate cakes du jour. After dinner, you can take a leisurely stroll through the national wildlife refuge nearby.

Tim's Rivershore
Restaurant & Crab House

1510 Cherry Hill Road
Dumfries, VA 22026
703-441-1375
www.timsrivershore.com

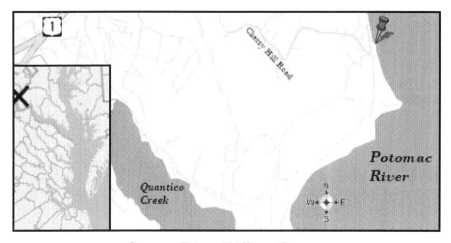

County: Prince William County
Open: Year Round
Latitude: N 38° 34' 8" ⚓ Longitude: W 77° 15' 44"
Body of Water: Potomac River
Dockage: Yes
Driving Distance: Richmond: 83 miles,
Norfolk: 168 miles, Washington, DC: 34 miles

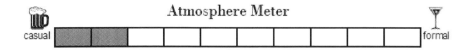

Tim's Rivershore is a piece of cake to reach by boat. You can pull up at the 400-foot pier, or drop anchor and take the water shuttle into shore. But driving is quite an adventure.

After winding your way through the Virginia countryside, you come upon railroad tracks and your GPS might try to convince you that you're in the middle of the Potomac River. Never fear. Just take a left on the gravel road and look for the sign with a big crab and Tim.

No matter how you arrive, you'll be glad you came to this crab house that specializes in escaping from the daily grind. The spectacular waterfront view serves as a backdrop to red and yellow palm trees, strings of tiki lights, and swaying sea grass. You can relax with a cool drink on the wooden deck, three outdoor bars, or the tiki beach. Inside, nautical decorations are hung on walls painted white with red accents.

Locally caught crabs are the menu's best pick, with steamed shrimp, oysters, and mussels also weighing in as popular dishes. Pulled pork, juicy burgers, and rockfish sandwiches complete the casual fare. Tim's Rivershore Mud Pie and root beer floats are irresistible after-dinner treats.

When bands play on summer nights, this place really rocks. But if it gets too crowded for your taste, you can visit its sister restaurant, Tim's II in Fairview Beach.

Tim's II at Fairview Beach
Restaurant & Crab House

5411 Pavilion Drive
King George, VA 22485
540-775-7500
www.tims2.com

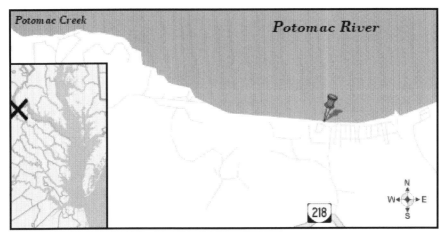

County: Charles County, MD, and King George County, VA
Open: Year Round
Latitude: N 38° 19' 52" ⚓ Longitude: W 77° 14' 49"
Body of Water: Potomac River
Dockage: Yes
Driving Distance: Richmond: 72 miles,
Norfolk: 158 miles, Washington, DC: 63 miles

Atmosphere Meter

casual 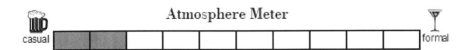 formal

Consider yourself lucky if you hit Tim's II for a late lunch and the waitress invites you to help feed the catfish. As she tosses chunks of hush puppies and stale buns from the pier, the water churns with tails and fins and whiskers. When the fish frenzy is almost over, two massive carp — named Bubba and Bubbette — slowly surface to suck up their meal.

This unforgettable scene is a rare treat, because Tim's II is usually so busy that Bubba and his pals prefer the quiet water under the deck. Since it was spun off from Tim's Rivershore in Dumfries in 2002, this rustic crab house has been a magnet for fun-seekers around the Bay.

From its massive wooden deck, you can listen to live bands or join the festivities at one of its annual events, such as the Jet Ski Poker Run, Not On the 4th Fireworks, or Our Radar Run, where "officials" time the speed of your boat.

Or you can sit beneath its red and yellow palm trees, enjoying a casual meal garnished with panoramic views of the Potomac. Starters (Lures & Nibbles) include crab dip, wings, and fried pickles. Pulled pork, burgers, and fish tacos are sandwich highlights. Carnivores can indulge in steaks accompanied by potato salad, baked beans, or coleslaw. But your best bet is ordering local seafood steamers packed with crab, shrimp, oysters, or mussels, and washed down with an icy cold beer.

Rick's on the River Restaurant & Bar

6338 Riverview Drive
King George, VA 22485
540-775-4600
www.ricksontheriverfvb.com

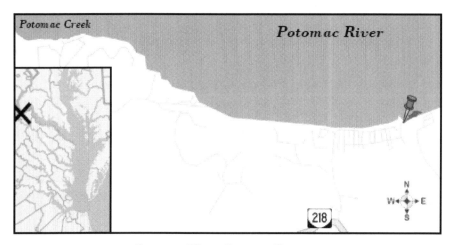

County: King George County
Open: Seasonal
Latitude: N 38° 19' 53" ⚓ Longitude: W 77° 14' 6"
Body of Water: Potomac River
Dockage: Yes
Driving Distance: Richmond: 73 miles,
Norfolk: 158 miles, Washington, DC: 62 miles

Atmosphere Meter

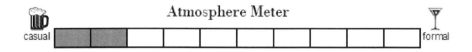

casual · · · · · · · · · · formal

If you want to get away for a perfect day trip, head over to Rick's on the River. Red, blue, and yellow Adirondack chairs insist that you get lazy and watch boats cruise around the Bay.

Two outside tiki bars serve plenty of drinks to keep you hydrated on a hot summer afternoon.

The waterfront property is surprisingly large, with a fenced-in beach area for the kids and lots of dockage to tie up boats. Live music, karaoke nights, and bikini contests add a little spice to weekends. Sunsets are simply spectacular.

When you get hungry and need a break from the sun, take a seat on the outside deck that's covered with a long awning and decorated with scores of colorful fishing buoys.

The creative menu can accommodate just about any craving. You can start with bacon-wrapped scallops, steamed shrimp, six flavors of chicken wings, or jalapeño poppers filled with warm cream cheese. No-filler crab cakes, broiled rockfish, and beer batter shrimp fried to a golden brown are local favorites. Not in a seafood mood? Try a burger with hand-cut fries, a chicken club with thick slices of bacon, or the Beez Kneez Steak 'n Cheese with Cheez Whiz on a toasted hoagie roll.

But be sure to save room for a treat from the specialty drink menu. Its tropical concoctions can induce an island state of mind: Bahama Blue, String Bikini, Malibu Wipeout, or Key Lime Cocktail (the glass is rimmed with graham cracker crumbs!).

Wilkerson's Seafood Restaurant

3900 McKinney Boulevard
Colonia Beach, VA 22443
804-224-7117
www.wilkersonsseafoodrestaurant.com

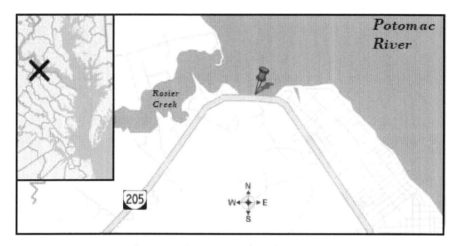

County: Westmoreland County
Open: Year Round; closed between Thanksgiving and New Year's
Latitude: N 38° 16' 22" ⚓ Longitude: W 76° 59' 42"
Body of Water: Potomac River
Dockage: No
Driving Distance: Richmond: 71 miles,
Norfolk: 157 miles, Washington, DC: 62 miles

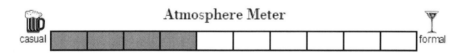

Atmosphere Meter

casual   formal

Since 1946, the Wilkerson family has been steaming crabs and shrimp at their restaurant on the Potomac. The building sustained heavy damage during Hurricane Isabel, but recent renovations have given this place a clean, open feel.

Crab pots, fish nets, and nautical artifacts greet you at the front door. Mounted trophy fish hang on the pale wooded walls, but the expansive view of the river is the main attraction in the dining room. Even if you only order a beer at the bar, you receive a basket of crispy warm hush puppies served with butter and honey.

A crab dotting the "i" on the sign outside says that this restaurant cares about seafood. Local crab cakes, spiced shrimp, and fried oysters are your best bets on the menu. Other specialties are rockfish and prime rib. A salad bar and seafood buffet allow you to pick your favorites veggies.

After dinner, go explore the resort town of Colonial Beach. Vacationers since the mid-1800s have traveled here by boat, but today you can cruise around in golf carts to see quaint Victorian homes, summer cottages, and antique shops. Music festivals and fishing tournaments draw big summer crowds. History buffs can take tours of Alexander Graham Bell's summer home and George Washington's birthplace. Or you can just take lay out a blanket and enjoy a hot summer day at the beach.

Riverboat on the Potomac

301 Beach Terrace
Colonial Beach, VA 22443
804-224-7055
www.theriverboat.net

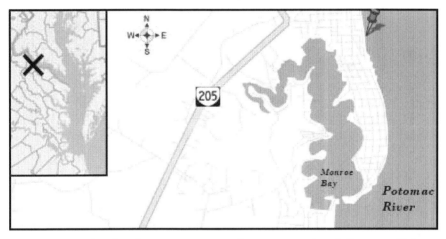

County: Charles County, MD, and Westmoreland County, VA
Open: Year Round
Latitude: N 38° 15' 11" ⚓ Longitude: W 76° 57' 39"
Body of Water: Potomac River
Dockage: Yes
Driving Distance: Richmond: 73 miles,
Norfolk: 159 miles, Washington, DC: 64 miles

Atmosphere Meter

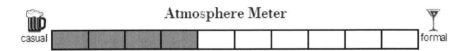

casual   formal

    Feeling lucky? Then come place your bets at Riverboat on the Potomac. It's a mini Las Vegas open seven days a week for Keno, lottery, and off-track betting. For daily specials, this casino runs a brunch buffet Sunday, discount drafts and rail drinks on Monday, prime rib on Tuesday, Wednesday and

Saturday Texas Hold 'em Tournaments, Thursday Bar Pong, and Riverboat Idol or karaoke on Friday.

Whether you arrive by car, boat, or golf cart, you can't miss this huge gray building on the waterfront. A long wooden bar stretches the length of the OTB parlor where gamblers stare intently at horse races on TVs. The dining room's white linen tables provide a quiet retreat from gaming, and the outdoor deck helps gamblers contemplate winning strategies while taking in a spectacular view of the river.

The Tiki Bar's pale turquoise walls and island decorations offer a relaxed change of pace from the main betting venue. You can blow off steam with a few games of Skeeball or take a leisurely stroll on the pier. The banquet rooms have plenty of space for special events and private parties.

The menu's strong suit is local seafood with specialties like Snockered Shrimp steamed in dark beer, fried oysters, and parmesan-crusted flounder. The sandwich board is flush with nautical-theme choices like The Rudder (grilled corn beef reuben) and The Paddle Wheel (North Carolina-style pulled BBQ pork). And meat lovers will lick their chops over the slow-roasted prime rib, juicy New York strip steaks, or crispy pieces of Southern fried chicken.

High Tides on the Potomac
& Black Pearl Tiki Bar

205 Taylor Street
Colonial Beach, VA 22443
804-224-8433
www.hightidez.com

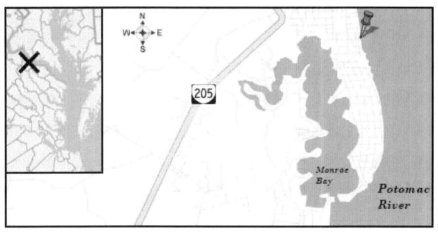

County: Westmoreland County
Open: Year Round
Latitude: N 38° 15' 6" ⚓ Longitude: W 76° 57' 41"
Body of Water: Potomac River
Dockage: Yes, at Colonial Beach Municipal Town Pier
Driving Distance: Richmond: 73 miles,
Norfolk: 159 miles, Washington, DC: 64 miles

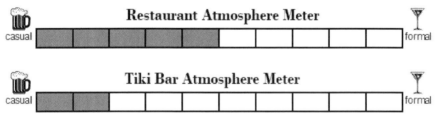

High Tides on the Potomac is located on the boardwalk of
the second longest public beach in Virginia. Whether you're

seated on the outdoor deck or the inside dining room, you're wowed by a stunning view of the water.

The restaurant has a lovely open feel, thanks to a vaulted ceiling and walls of tall windows framed in blond wood. The décor is kept simple to showcase the seaside scene of people strolling on the boardwalk. An 18th century pirate statue at the front door dutifully holds a daily specials board but keeps his unpatched eye on the Black Pearl Tiki Bar where patrons groove in the sand to bands under strings of white lights.

The food here is quite good. Steaks, burgers, and chicken are grilled to perfection, while signature soups are served in bread bowls. Seafood ranges from Malibu Coconut Shrimp to Seafood Combo with crab cakes, shrimp, and scallops.

If you order local oysters, you'll nibble on a nugget of local history that rivaled the mayhem of the Wild West. Colonial Beach was a hotbed during the Oyster Wars of the 1900s. Over-harvesting reduced the oyster beds to such a level that violence erupted all around the Bay. This area was a haven for Virginia watermen, called the Mosquito Fleet, who illegally dredged oysters, then used high-speed boats to evade Maryland police and escape into the safety of Monroe Bay.

The Lighthouse Restaurant & Lounge

11 Monroe Bay Avenue
Colonial Beach, VA 22443
804-224-7580
www.colonialbeachlighthouse.com

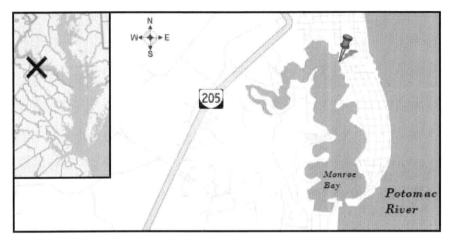

County: Westmoreland County
Open: Year Round
Latitude: N 38° 14' 57" Longitude: W 76° 57' 57"
Body of Water: Monroe Bay off the Potomac River
Dockage: Yes
Driving Distance: Richmond: 73 miles,
Norfolk: 159 miles, Washington, DC: 64 miles

Atmosphere Meter

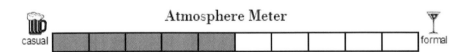

casual   formal

Since the glory days of steamboats in the 1800s, sun lovers have flocked to Colonial Beach to romp in the sand or climb aboard boats for world-class fishing. Swarms of tourists and long waits for restaurant seating are inevitable. But if you go off the beaten path, The Lighthouse can help you escape the crowds and have a delightful waterfront experience.

This family-owned place is on the flip-side of town along the shore of Monroe Bay, where watermen unload their daily catch at the seafood market next door. The warm décor pays tribute to their labors. A mural around the bar borrows the vibrant colors of sunset to show a fishing boat returning to the dock after a long day on the water. A spectacular marlin hangs on one of the dining room's amber walls. And the stern of a family boat, *The Shady Lady*, is built into the bar's wall, because it held too many fond memories to be discarded.

The menu echoes the fruits of the Bay with a fine lineup of seafood. You can begin with steamed clams, mussels, and shrimp, or choose crab stuffed into mushrooms or swirled into a creamy dip. Standouts include Rockfish Oscar topped with asparagus tips, lump crab, and hollandaise, and Caribbean Salmon coated with jerk spices and mango chutney. Land entrees feature savory New York strip steaks and Lighthouse Chicken covered with lump crab, country ham, and brown butter. Hearty sandwiches of soft-shell crabs, pulled pork, and burgers complete the casual fare.

Dockside Restaurant
& Blue Heron Pub

1787 Castlewood Drive
Colonial Beach, VA 22443
804-224-8726
www.docksiderestaurantandblueheronpub.com

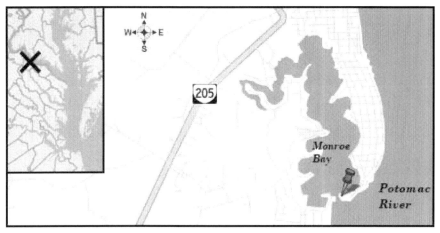

County: Westmoreland County
Open: Year Round
Latitude: N 38° 13' 49" ⚓ Longitude: W 76° 57' 51"
Body of Water: Potomac River
Dockage: Yes
Driving Distance: Richmond: 75 miles,
Norfolk: 161 miles, Washington, DC: 66 miles

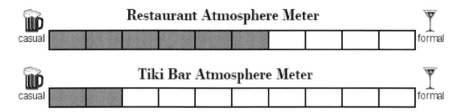

Seafood served with a hearty dash of history is what you
find at Dockside Restaurant and Blue Heron Pub. Built in

1932 as an oyster-shucking house, the structure floated away in a 1933 flood, but mules hauled it back to where it sits today. In 1640, George Washington's great-great grandfather John was the first mate on a British trading ship that sank offshore. After swimming to safety, he met a local gal named Anne Pope. They married and made their home here.

During the Civil War, Confederate spies used Monroe Bay (named for the 5th president's great-grandfather) to slip into Virginia and bring info to the officers. After a 1985 storm, beach combers found skeleton feet sticking out of the sand. Forensics revealed the bones belong to 19th Century oystermen who had been shanghaied and buried in shallow waters. The house ghost is allegedly one of the ill-fated workers.

The restaurant's dark green and blue walls, paintings of Bay scenes, and crackling fireplace create a pleasant ambience for dining on high-quality local seafood, steaks, and chicken. The tiki bar's eclectic array of sea creatures, fish nets, and vintage signs sets the tone for upbeat fun. Bands play on weekends. The waterfront deck and sandy area have a lively Caribbean feel with neon green, purple, and pink beach chairs that dare you to relax and enjoy a summer sunset. All in all, it's a wonderful place to get away.

Coles Point Tavern

850 Salisbury Park Road
Coles Point, VA 22442
804-472-3856
www.colespointtavern.com

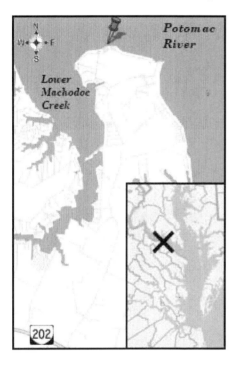

County: St. Mary's County,
  MD, and Westmoreland
  County, VA

Open: Year Round

Latitude: N 38° 9' 11"

Longitude: W 76° 37' 52"

Body of Water: Potomac River

Dockage: Yes

Driving Distance:
  Richmond: 74 miles
  Norfolk: 122 miles
  Washington, DC: 96 miles

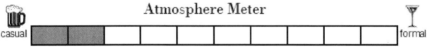

Atmosphere Meter

casual | | | | | | | | | | formal

You might wonder why Coles Point Tavern's address is in Virginia but it's located in St. Mary's County, Maryland. It's part of the Bay's quirky history that goes back to the 1600s. When King Charles I gave a chunk of the Virginia Colony to Cecil Calvert of Baltimore to establish Maryland, the monarch drew the boundary line along the southern bank of the

Potomac River. For centuries, the border has been contested. Even George Washington built a herring hatchery at Mount Vernon on the Potomac and never paid Maryland for using its waters. But the state line remains unchanged, so at Coles Point you park your car in Virginia or dock your boat in Maryland.

Why was the restaurant built on pilings in the Potomac in 1953? Back then, gambling was made legal in Maryland but not Virginia. Westmoreland County citizens wanted a piece of the action, so they put casinos on river barges with piers that allowed guests to walk from the shore to test Lady Luck.

Today inside the time-worn pub, Keno and lottery tickets still hold a place at the bar. When bands play in the back room, patrons shift from gambling to dancing. The décor mixes crabs, pirates, and tiki into a rustic house of fun.

You can order food to go or enjoy a simple meal on the 120-foot wood deck with a view that's hard to beat. Baskets of fried shrimp, chicken tenders, and wings come with fries. Sandwich selections include burgers, crab cakes, Philly cheese steaks, or a Ragged Point Club with your pick of deli meat.

AC's Café & Sports Grill

607 Plantation Drive
Coles Point, VA 22422
804-472-5528
www.acssportsgrill.com

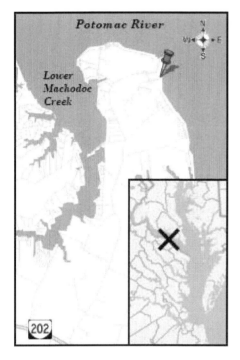

County: Westmoreland County

Open: Year Round

Latitude: N 38° 8' 33"

Longitude: W 76° 36' 53"

Body of Water: Potomac River

Dockage: Yes

Driving Distance:
  Richmond: 74 miles
  Norfolk: 122 miles
  Washington, DC: 96 miles

Atmosphere Meter

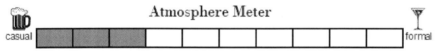

casual   formal

Sometimes you're not in the mood to watch your favorite sports team alone. It just feels better to exchange high-fives when they're up or complain about the officials when they're down. That's the best time to join the gang at AC's Café & Sports Grill. This local hangout is an oasis of sports revelry amidst the gentle countryside of Virginia's Northern Neck. If you drive in from the west, you pass the birthplaces of George Washington and Robert E. Lee. Boaters know they found the right place when they hear laughter erupting from the shore of the Potomac River.

The two-tiered waterfront deck's view of the marina is spectacular. Hanging from the covered deck's rafters are banners for the Orioles, Redskins, Ravens, Terrapins, and Cavaliers, which say everyone's welcome to cheer here.

Inside the main bar, a pair of American flags and strings of colorful sports hats add a splash of color to the wooden walls. You can bet on the horses with OTB or watch multiple events on the 19 big TVs mounted beneath the ceiling. A fireplace in the side room accented with NASCAR paraphernalia keeps race fans warm in the off-season. NFL enthusiasts are treated to a special buffet during playoffs.

The menu focuses on home-style comfort food cooked with local ingredients. Pub fare of burgers, sandwiches, salads, and seafood are tasty munchies for watching games at this energetic spot along the water.

The Mooring Restaurant

347 Allen Point Lane
Kinsale, VA 22488
804-472-2044
www.portkinsale.com/dining.aspx

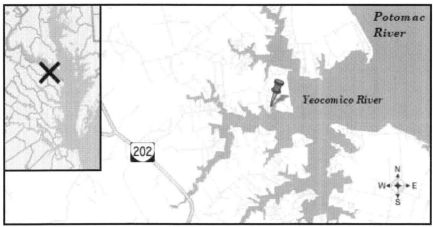

County: Westmoreland County
Open: Year Round
Latitude: N 38° 1' 51"   Longitude: W 76° 33' 28"
Body of Water: Western Branch of the Yeocomico River off the
Potomac River
Dockage: Yes
Driving Distance: Richmond: 67 miles,
Norfolk: 115 miles, Washington, DC: 97 miles

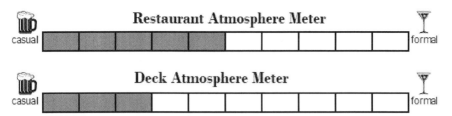

What do you get when you combine two popular cuisines —
Chesapeake Bay and Italian — in one fabulous location? The
Mooring Restaurant. It's been a Northern Neck staple since

1965, but new owners took the helm in 2005 and created a new dining experience. They amassed a collection of regional wines and started making everything from scratch. Bread and pizza dough are kneaded in-house, sausages are stuffed in the kitchen, and meatballs taste like somebody got their hands on your grandmother's secret recipe.

Grazing through the antipasto station in the buffet area is like taking a Tuscan vacation. Flash-fried calamari with aioli sauce and creamy crab dip get meals moving in the right direction. And what could be better than sitting with friends and peeling a pound of shrimp? Oysters topped with spinach, cheese, and pancetta are baked until they bubble.

Home-made pasta appeals to fish and meat lovers alike with standouts such as blackened chicken alfredo and the Chef's Shrimp Special with capers, sun-dried tomatoes, and basil in a lemony white wine sauce. Seafood pizza topped with shrimp, clams, and calamari is a circle of cheesy fun.

With so much delicious food at your fingertips, don't forget to stroll around the place. You'll find the Lucky Lady, a 54-year old boat turned into a deck bar. On weekends you can kick back and listen to live bands play under the stars. And down at the marina, you can check out a century-old skipjack called the *Virginia W.*

Kinsale Harbour Restaurant

285 Kinsale Road
Kinsale, VA 22488
804-472-2514

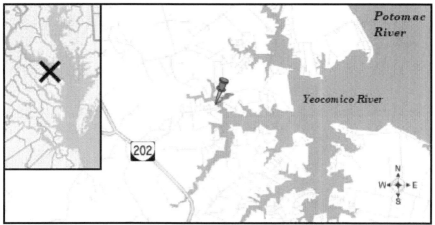

County: Westmoreland County
Open: Seasonal
Latitude: N 38° 1' 52" Longitude: W 76° 34' 36"
Body of Water: Kinsale Branch off the Yeocomico River off the
Potomac River
Dockage: Yes
Driving Distance: Richmond: 66 miles,
Norfolk: 114 miles, Washington, DC: 96 miles

Atmosphere Meter

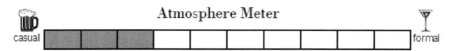

casual   formal

When you want to escape the hectic pace of urban living, take a spin over to Kinsale Harbor Restaurant. It's located near the sleepy harbor town of Kinsale, which is steeped in history. During colonial times, the harbor was a commercial hub for trips across the Atlantic to England. By the 1800s, residents worked at the tomato canning plant or fished the local waters. Chesapeake steamboats delivered goods and guests, and the James Adams Floating Theater stopped on a regular basis. Today, graceful Victorian homes and a small museum serve as reminders of the region's colorful heyday.

The restaurant sits next to a bridge that spans the river. The waterfront deck overlooks a charming marina, and a rustic tiki bar upstairs adds strings of lights and a touch of the islands to this tranquil rural scene. Sunsets from this vantage point are marvelous.

Inside, the dining area hums with locals grabbing a bite to eat with their neighbors. The walls are painted a creamy white with cherry red accents. Nautical items hang under navy blue curtains, and the atmosphere is casual.

The menu celebrates the local watermen's bounty. Crab cakes are plump, shrimp are sweet and pink, and oysters taste like they were just pulled from the river. Sandwiches, soups, and salads taste home-made.

Tommy's Restaurant

729 Main Street
Reedville, VA 22539
804-453-4666
www.tommysrestaurant.net

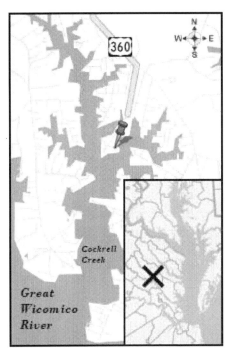

County: Northumberland County

Open: Year Round

Latitude: N 37° 50' 25"

Longitude: W 76° 16' 36"

Body of Water: Cockrell Creek off the Great Wicomico River

Dockage: No

Driving Distance:
  Richmond: 85 miles
  Norfolk: 97 miles
  Washington, DC: 119 miles

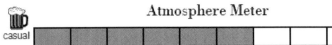

Atmosphere Meter

casual | | | | | | | | | | | formal

Reedville's Main Street is lined with exquisite Victorian homes that were built in the late 1800s by sea captains and owners of fish processing plants. Nestled among these architectural treasures is Tommy's Restaurant. The beautiful old house was a cannery at the turn of the century, a general store during the 1950s, and transformed into a fine-dining restaurant two decades ago. Its red roof and white walls accentuate the building's graceful lines. The porch's understated country charm lures you into an outdoor seat on summer nights. The golden brown woodwork, antique stained glass, and vintage nautical pictures give the inside dining rooms a cozy feel when the temperature drops.

Wednesday through Saturday evenings is when the chefs fire up the ovens in the kitchen. The menu begins with an assortment of tasty starters: fried oysters, calamari, and baked brie with mango chutney. Seafood selections include crab cakes, fried soft-shells, grilled rockfish, and jumbo shrimp. Tender steaks, rack of lamb, and sautéed veal liver are on hand for meat lovers. Desserts are baked in-house and vary daily. Somehow everything tastes better in this elegant romantic setting.

If you want to learn more about this quaint town, visit the Reedville Watermen's Museum that's located in the historic district within walking distance of Tommy's. Exhibits tell the story of this area's maritime heritage, watermen, and commercial fishing industry.

The Crazy Crab Restaurant

902 Main Street
Reedville, VA 22539
804-453-6789
www.reedvillemarina.com

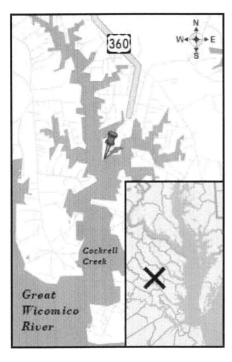

County: Northumberland
County

Open: Year Round

Latitude: N 37° 50' 16"

Longitude: W 76° 16' 46"

Body of Water: Cockrell Creek
off the Great Wicomico River

Dockage: Yes

Driving Distance:
Richmond: 85 miles
Norfolk: 97 miles
Washington, DC: 119 miles

Atmosphere Meter

casual | | | | | | | | | | formal

The name, Crazy Crab, is a bit misleading. Rather than meeting a mad crustacean or bi-polar bivalve on the premises, you're greeted by people who are committed to serving daily catch from the local waters. With the exception of a few entrees from the shore — Delmonico steak, prime rib, pork BBQ, and chicken in a portabella sauce — seafood is the main

---

attraction. Appetizer highlights include tender steamed clams, creamy crab dip in a bread bowl, and tuna medallions with Caribbean relish. Menu choices read like the Who's Who of seafood favorites. Crab cakes are made traditional Chesapeake style with only a whisper of filler. Flounder is stuffed with a silky crab imperial, and the Captain's Platter is laden with shrimp, sea scallops, crab, and fish.

The atmosphere is pleasant and upbeat. Graceful wrought-iron and glass chandeliers brighten the mood. Creamy white interior walls are garnished with black fishnet curtains and pictures of watermen in vintage sailing vessels.

From the outside deck you can see (and sometimes smell) the nearby fish oil processing plant. It represents an industry that played a key role in the region's history. Elijah Reed, a Maine sea captain, rolled into town back in 1874 hoping to develop commercial fishing for massive schools of Atlantic menhaden. These tiny, buttery fish were plentiful here and harvested by the millions to produce oil, fertilizer, animal feed, and even lipstick. Reedville residents built their waterfront town on the menhaden fishing business.

Leadbelly's Restaurant

252 Polly Cove Road
Reedville, VA 22539
804-453-5002

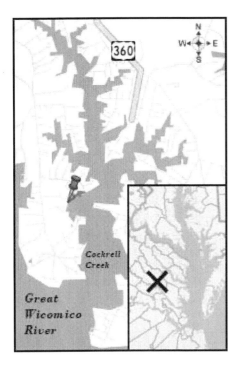

County: Northumberland
County

Open: Year Round

Latitude: N 37° 49' 57"

Longitude: W 76° 17' 11"

Body of Water: Cockrell Creek
off the Great Wicomico River

Dockage: Yes

Driving Distance:
Richmond: 84 miles
Norfolk: 97 miles
Washington, DC: 119 miles

  Atmosphere Meter

casual   formal

If this book gave an award for Most Energetic Décor, Leadbelly's would be a serious contender. The plain gray building offers only one clue that lots of fun is happening here — a sign with a big grinning frog flashing a peace sign. But once you step inside, you're treated to a collage of bright flags, twinkle lights, tiki grass, a giant yellow sun, and a crab boat mural around the bar. Booth seats are covered with hundreds of colorful duct tape swatches (this kept the kids busy while owners got ready to open in 2011). The screened porch elevates the tiki feel with banana leaves painted on the walls, thatched trim across the ceiling, and a 10-foot shark mounted above the dartboard. It's creative and vibrant, yet homey.

Even though a stuffed rooster clings to the top of the daily specials board, food here is not all fun and games. Shedding tanks around back harbor molting crabs, and working boats are docked at the marina next door. It's a clear sign that the seafood is fresh, local, and delicious.

Frog legs, spicy or mild, are the signature dish. But knowing that shedding tanks are just outside makes it nearly impossible to skip a soft-shell sandwich or crab cake. Oysters baked in lemon garlic butter with bacon bits and cheddar are addictive. Carnivores can opt for steak, burgers, pulled pork, or liver with onions. The Little Belly's menu dishes out pizza, hot dogs, and chicken tenders for the youngsters. And if the kids get restless while you savor your last bites, they can draw on a chalkboard slate wall, grab a water pistol on the porch, or toss beanbags near the parking lot. All in all, it's hard to find a better place to spend a summer day.

Horn Harbor House
Seafood Restaurant

836 Horn Harbor Road
Burgess, VA 22432
804-453-3351

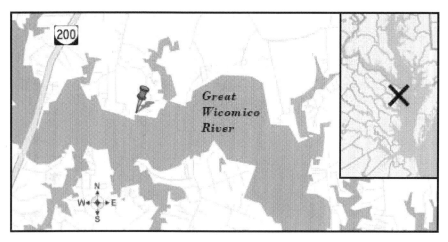

County: Northumberland County
Open: Year Round
Latitude: N 37° 51' 2" ⚓ Longitude: W 76° 20' 54"
Body of Water: Great Wicomico River
Dockage: Yes
Driving Distance: Richmond: 81 miles,
Norfolk: 91 miles, Washington, DC: 116 miles

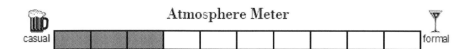

Sometimes you need to take a chance and go off the
beaten path to find authentic seafood. But the joy of discovery
— and a really good crab cake — can make an adventurous

trip worthwhile. That's the case with Horn Harbor. It's tucked away on a remote part of the Northern Neck, surrounded by a marina, campground, and swimming area. The rolling landscape is idyllic for nature enthusiasts.

It's a big place with a unique rustic style that looks like a fusion of an old boat house and a barn. Nautical and farm items are strewn around the grounds, and a buxom blonde figurehead stares down from the roof. Wooden booths on the deck give a close-up view of the marina. Watermen's tools of the trade — oyster tongs, fish nets, and crab pots — hang from the dining room walls. The casual, easy-going atmosphere makes it a favorite haunt for locals.

The menu offers a seemingly endless selection of fresh local catch. The Seafood Sampler rounds up all the usual suspects, including shrimp, scallops, oysters, crab, and calamari, and fortifies them with home-made marina sauce. Crabs are cooked every way imaginable from broiled cakes to buttery Norfolk. Oysters plucked from the river nearby are lightly breaded and fried to a golden crisp.

Not in a seafood mood? Then sample the Italian dishes of spaghetti and pizza. Or sink you teeth into a juicy steak, thick hamburger, White Marble Farm pork chops, or Philly cheese steak. Just try to leave room for desserts like key lime pie and banana pudding. They're terrific.

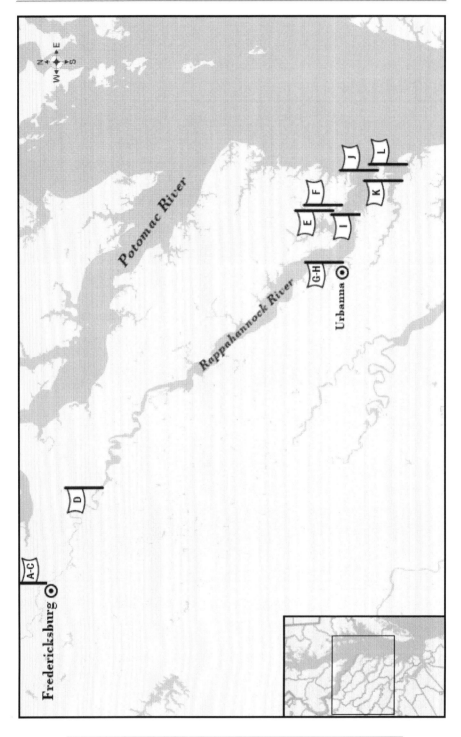

Rappahannock River

TruLuv's

1101 Sophia Street
Fredericksburg, VA 22401
540-373-6500
www.truluvs.net

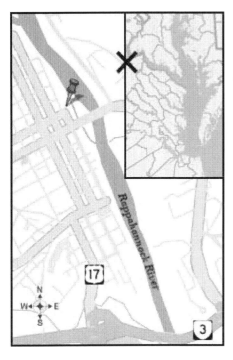

County: Fredericksburg (city)

Open: Year Round

Latitude: N 38° 18' 19"

Longitude: W 77° 27' 33"

Body of Water: Rappahannock
River

Dockage: No

Driving Distance:
Richmond: 57 miles
Norfolk: 143 miles
Washington, DC: 53 miles

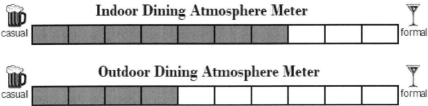

TruLuv's has a warm heart for three things: dogs, music, and good food. This handsome eatery creates a special spot for each part of its holy trinity. Pups with leashes are welcome to join the fun on the back patio overlooking the river. It's got plenty of space and a nice grassy area for an afternoon doggie nap. Rock and roll takes center stage in the bar. On its rich red walls hang black-framed posters of music greats such as Janice Joplin, Jimi Hendrix, Nat King Cole, and Miles Davis. Live bands fill the room with energy.

The dining room finds a happy medium between the lively bar and patio. Its walls and graceful arches are colored in soft amber earth tones, and a brick fireplace crackles near the back. White linens blanket the tables, and a petite palm tree adds a splash of soothing green to the scene. The kitchen serves a nice assortment of modern bistro fare. Shrimp comes with grits, fried Blue Point oysters are a crispy bliss, and sea scallops are gently seared. Filet mignon is topped with bacon and gorgonzola. Bread pudding finishes a lovely meal.

Directly across the river is a must-see historic mansion called Chatham Manor. Originally built for a plantation owner, it was occupied by Union forces during the Civil War. Lincoln discussed battle strategies with General McDowell under its roof. Clara Barton tended to wounded soldiers, and Walt Whitman searched for his injured brother here.

The Happy Clam
at Barefoot Green's

1017 Sophia Street
Fredericksburg, VA 22401
540-899-0140

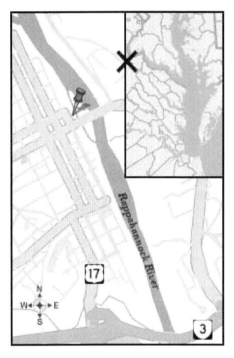

County: Fredericksburg (city)

Open: Year Round

Latitude: N 38° 18' 17"

Longitude: W 77° 27' 32"

Body of Water: Rappahannock
  River

Dockage: No

Driving Distance:
  Richmond: 57 miles
  Norfolk: 143 miles
  Washington, DC: 53 miles

Atmosphere Meter

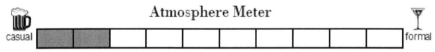

casual | | | | | | | | | | formal

    In Fredericksburg's historic district on the banks of the Rappahannock River is a little seafood house with lots of crabs, oysters, starfish, and ocean waves painted all over its walls. It used to be called Barefoot's, but the sign on top of the roof now reads The Happy Clam. In June 2012 new owners came to town because Hurricane Isabel washed away the original Happy Clam Restaurant in Colonial Beach.

The outdoor wooden deck provides an ideal spot for picking steamed crabs and watching people stroll along the street. The décor inside is casual, and walls are painted olive green with a bright yellow trim. The dining area only has room for about 10 tables, but it has a cozy neighborhood feel.

The building also houses a seafood market where you can grab carry-out fish and produce to prepare at home. But you might want to eat on-site and let the cooks do all the work. They specialize in fresh, no-frills seafood, prepared to order in traditional Chesapeake fashion.

Crab cakes with almost no filler are gently pan-fried. Creamy New England clam chowder is overpopulated with tender bivalves, and shrimp are steamed to perfection. Hush puppies bring a savory sweetness to each plate. If you're feeling more like a carnivore than a seafood fan, you can choose burgers or chicken. And this family-friendly place offers dishes like chicken tenders for children that want to come along to explore the area's latest seafood hot spot.

Brock's Riverside Grill

503 Sophia Street
Fredericksburg, VA 22401
540-370-1820
www.brocksgrill.com

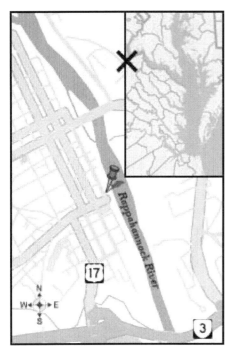

County: Fredericksburg (city)

Open: Year Round

Latitude: N 38° 17' 57"

Longitude: W 77° 27' 19"

Body of Water: Rappahannock
  River

Dockage: No

Driving Distance:
  Richmond: 57 miles
  Norfolk: 143 miles
  Washington, DC: 53 miles

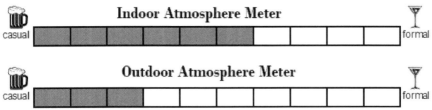

Visiting Old Town Fredericksburg gives you a chance to walk the streets where Washington, Jefferson, and James Monroe used to stroll. From Colonial to Civil War times, historic sites await you. Architectural treasures — more than

350 of which were built before 1870 — are around every corner. Many are home to music stores, boutiques, pubs, and gift shops. On these streets, contemporary commerce blends easily with Old World brick and mortar.

This marriage of past and present gives Brock's a special charm. The restaurant was established in 1999, but the building was built well over a century ago. Stained glass, antique furniture, and vintage photos accentuate the graceful lines of the dining room and bar. The outdoor deck sports a simpler, modern design that matches its lively atmosphere. Views of the stone-arched bridge over the Rappahannock seem to pull everything together.

The menu infuses seafood and steaks with Southwest flavors. Entrée standouts include mahi-mahi with mango-chutney relish and grilled salmon with honey-red wine glaze. Crab cakes are fresh and plump. Juicy prime rib, blackened chicken alfredo, and St. Louis-style ribs make your mouth water. And specialty cocktails, such as the Firefly Martini or the "Best Bloody Mary in Town," should not be overlooked.

Buster's Place

136 Main Street
Port Royal, VA 22535
804-742-5078
www.bustersplaceva.com

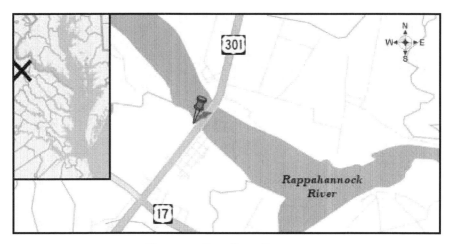

County: Caroline County
Open: Year Round
Latitude: N 38° 10' 23" ⚓ Longitude: W 77° 11' 25"
Body of Water: Rappahannock River
Dockage: Yes
Driving Distance: Richmond: 55 miles,
Norfolk: 122 miles, Washington, DC: 65 miles

Atmosphere Meter

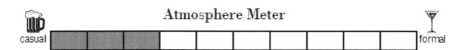

High on the bank above the Rappahannock River sits a one-story gray building that's home to Buster's Place. If you dine inside, gaze out the round porthole windows at the bar and feel like you're in a vintage cruise ship. The best seats in the house are the window booths that offer a view of traffic cruising across the bridge and boats pulling up to the dock.

The blue awning over the outside deck offers cool shade on hot August afternoons. A string of lights along the tiny tiki bar lend a touch of cheer after the sun goes down, and live music fills the air on weekends.

Casual fare is prepared with a nod to the South, where fried green tomatoes appear on plates with hot crabs and spiced shrimp. Po' boys overstuffed with oysters, clams, or scallops are the darlings of the sandwich board, and entrees showcase crispy hush puppies with crab cakes, soft-shells, or clam strips. Landlubbers can sink their teeth into a juicy rib eye steak, tender chicken breasts, or spaghetti with meatballs.

When you leave Buster's and head into Port Royal, be on your best behavior. This quaint little town (pop. 170) knows how to deal with troublemakers. In 1865, John Wilkes Booth was fatally shot in Garrett's barn about two miles away from where you just picked crabs. A less famous villain met his maker two centuries earlier. During the late 1600s, this area was a favorite stomping ground for pirates, including a nefarious Frenchman named Monsieur Peuman. Local townsfolk, fed up with this marauder's thieving ways, chased him up a creek until his boat got stranded in shallow waters. They jumped on board, killed the privateer, and named the stream "Peumans End" as a warning to other scalawags.

Tides Inn

480 King Carter Drive
Irvington, VA 22480
804-438-4489
www.tidesinn.com

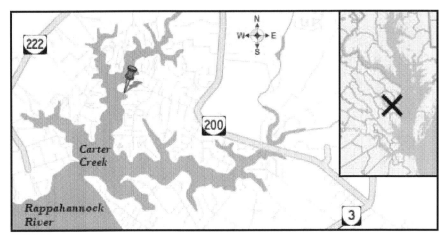

County: Lancaster County
Open: Year Round
Latitude: N 37° 39' 51" ⚓ Longitude: W 76° 25' 57"
Body of Water: Carter Creek off the Rappahannock River
Dockage: Yes
Driving Distance: Richmond: 69 miles,
Norfolk: 76 miles, Washington, DC: 125 miles

Atmosphere Meter

casual 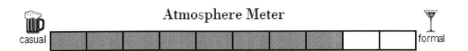 formal

    Most people think that Tides Inn is just a beautiful luxury resort. Well, that's partially true. Its gorgeous location along Carter Creek creates an idyllic spot for romantic weekend get-aways or special family gatherings. Several dining venues combine the bounty of the Bay with Northern Neck cuisine in distinctly different ways to accommodate everybody's mood and budget.

The Inn's centerpiece is the Chesapeake Club, with serene atmosphere and gourmet dining. Ingredients are local, seasonal, and garden fresh. Show-stealing starters: smoked salmon tartar with cucumber-wasabi dressing and Rappahannock oysters with pickled cucumber salsa. Main course highlights include jumbo lump crab cakes, Bay flounder tempura, and pan-seared Virginia scallops. Meat specialties include beef tenderloin tips in a mushroom cognac cream sauce and Southern fried chicken dusted with Old Bay.

At Commodore's waterfront restaurant, you can lounge poolside next to the creek and relax with signature tropical drinks such as the Lancaster Lemonade or Dark & Stormy. The casual menu features blue crab quesadillas, seafood salad sandwiches, oyster po' boys, and smoked turkey sandwiches made with brie, Smithfield ham, and apple butter. The recently renovated Golden Eagle Grill, located at the golf course, serves light fare of fresh salads, thick burgers, quiche, chicken wraps with pesto mayo, and a crispy onion ring tower. No matter where you dine, this place is worth the trip.

Willaby's Café

327 Old Ferry Road
White Stone, VA 22578
804-435-0000
www.willabys.com

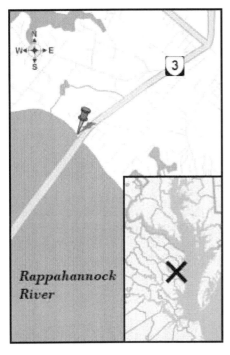

County: Lancaster County

Open: Year Round

Latitude: N 37° 38' 10"

Longitude: W 76° 24' 42"

Body of Water: Rappahannock River

Dockage: No

Driving Distance:
Richmond: 66 miles
Norfolk: 73 miles
Washington, DC: 126 miles

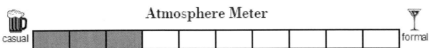

Atmosphere Meter

casual | | | | | | | | | | formal

"Wow!" is the word that people say when they catch a sunset at Willaby's. Mother Nature puts on a spectacular show when the sun makes its evening splash into the water. This location provides an ideal vantage point. A beach area with wooden picnic tables near the foot of the Norris Bridge lets you dig your toes in the sand while watching all the action along the Rappahannock River. Or you can take a seat on the outdoor deck and toast the view with a cool cocktail in hand. If you prefer indoor seating, the long wall of windows ensures you won't miss a moment of the sky's changing colors.

The restaurant is casual and laid-back. In peak summer months, crowds from nearby campgrounds stop by when they get tired of cooking meals over the fire. The menu here is heavy on seafood, featuring local oysters that you can eat fried, in a stew, or freshly shucked and presented on the half shell. Crabmeat is stuffed in mushroom caps, baked in a creamy dip, or packed into cakes for broiling. Steak, chicken breast, and pork BBQ keep everyone happy.

When your meal is over, take a moment to check out Willaby's unique building. It looks like an old-fashioned steamboat, which harkens back to the 1800s when water provided the primary means of travel from Baltimore to Norfolk and beyond. Hundreds of steamboats transported people, produce, and freight around the Bay until bridges were built, railroad tracks were laid, and cars became king of the road. To learn about these ships' glory days, visit the Steamboat Era Museum in nearby Irvington.

Payne's Crab House

10 Virginia Street
Urbanna, VA 23175
804-758-5301

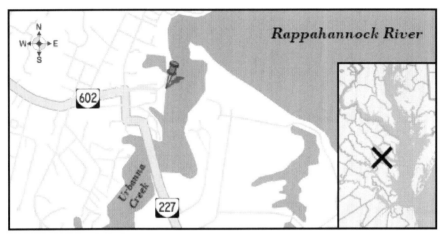

County: Middlesex County
Open: Seasonal, from May to November
Latitude: N 37° 38' 11" ⚓ Longitude: W 76° 34' 17"
Body of Water: Urbanna Creek off the Rappahannock River
Dockage: Yes
Driving Distance: Richmond: 56 miles,
Norfolk: 69 miles, Washington, DC: 123 miles

Atmosphere Meter

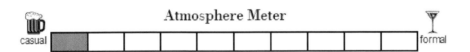

Payne's Crab House is by far one of the most authentic
Chesapeake gems you'll discover near the Bay. It takes you
back to a no-frills time when watermen and their families
spent long days pulling crabs from the water and cooking
their catch with neighbors. The tiny gray building sits on a

spot that's been home to crab houses since the 1880s. Blue crabs molt in shedding tanks around back along the shore. A few picnic tables under an awning provide outdoor seating.

The menu is simple: Crab cake sandwiches, fried soft-shells, steamed crabs, hot dogs, sodas, and oysters in season. But what makes this place extraordinary are the sisters who run it — Catherine Via and Beatrice Taylor.

Their father was a Tangier Island waterman who moved his family inland to Urbanna in 1933 after a devastating storm flooded the island. He bought the property in 1950 and put the girls to work in the family crab business. Today, they are the only females in Virginia commercially licensed to catch blue crabs. But it's their old-school hospitality and warmth that make this charming crab shack hum.

It's best to call before visiting these gals to make sure they're open. When your meal is done, hike up the hill and stroll around Urbanna. Its 543 residents welcome guests to their quaint shops and lovely old brick homes. The town erupts during the first week of November when it hosts up to 75,000 guests for the Virginia Oyster Festival with shucking contests, parades, music, and crafts.

All Fired Up
Smokehouse & Grill

25 Cross Street
Urbanna, VA 23175
804-286-9016

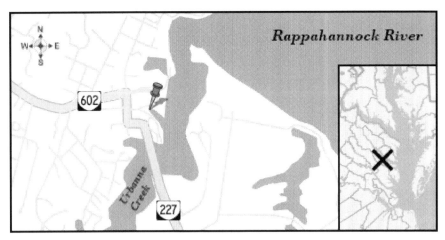

County: Middlesex County
Open: Year Round
Latitude: N 37° 38' 7" ⚓ Longitude: W 76° 34' 22"
Body of Water: Urbanna Creek off the Rappahannock River
Dockage: Yes
Driving Distance: Richmond: 56 miles,
Norfolk: 69 miles, Washington, DC: 123 miles

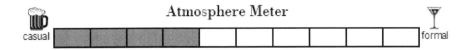

The massive black smokers parked near All Fired Up
leave no doubt that these folks are serious about slow-cooking
their food. The mouth-watering aroma pulls you into the

beige one-story building overlooking a marina. Its décor is casual and unique, with blond wood floors and fieldstone walls dividing the dining room into intimate spaces.

Since it opened in May 2011, the restaurant has churned out seafood dishes that range from traditional to highly creative. Fried flounder hoagies and oyster po' boys are crispy perfection. The grilled soft-shell reuben sandwich and salmon burger with havarti dill cheese prove it's okay to have fun and play with food. Grilled tuna steaks with fruit salsa offer a cool respite from the summer heat.

House-smoked corn beef, chicken, ribs, and pork are so juicy and tender that you don't need a knife. Some of the specialty dishes pile up enough tasty ingredients to earn Dagwood Bumstead's nod of approval. The BBQ Meal Wrap tucks pulled pork, baked beans, coleslaw, and fries into a soft flour tortilla. Captain's Burgers stack of juicy Angus beef, smoked bacon, crab dip, and Swiss cheese make you ask for extra napkins before your plate hits the table. The Flying Hawaiian stuffs a grilled chicken breast with coconut rice, ham, cilantro, and red peppers, and then tops the dish with grilled pineapple. And you don't dare to leave without trying fried mac and cheese.

Merroir Tasting Room

784 Locklies Creek Road
Topping, VA 23160
804-758-2871
www.rroysters.com

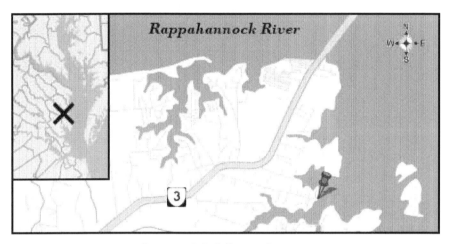

County: Middlesex County
Open: Seasonal
Latitude: N 37° 35' 38" Longitude: W 76° 26' 4"
Body of Water: Locklies Creek off the Rappahannock River
Dockage: Yes
Driving Distance: Richmond: 63 miles,
Norfolk: 70 miles, Washington, DC: 132 miles

Atmosphere Meter

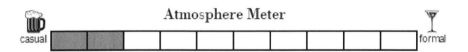

casual ⟶ formal

Merroir might call itself a tasting room, but seafood lovers think of this Chesapeake jewel as a little slice of heaven. It's part of the Rappahannock Oyster Co., owned by the Croxton family since 1899 and operated by two cousins who are determined to resurrect the local oyster population through

---

aquaculture farms. Rather than growing on the river bottom, these new-age bivalves are raised in cages the size of tabletops near the surface where water is cleaner and predators can't reach them. The result is healthier oysters that are available year-round in greater numbers.

Merroir is the retail outlet for buying these special oysters. You can take home a bag of them or try a sampling on site. The location is idyllic: a tiny house in the shade of an old tree in the middle of a lovely marina surrounded by piles of oyster shells and a languid landscape. You can sit on the porch or at a picnic table and watch the cook perform magic on his grill.

The menu encourages you to sample a variety of local wine, beer, and seafood. It's almost unthinkable to come here and not try the three types of oysters: Rappahannock, Stingray, and Olde Salt. You can choose raw or roasted. The Stuffin' Muffin mixes oysters in a moist stuffing then adds a layer of crisp from the grill. A bowl of lamb and clam stew fills your belly with warm savory spices, and crab cakes are plump and fresh. Soft-shell crabs arrive with green tomatoes and lemon thyme dressing. Rib eye steaks and pork tenderloin offer meaty alternatives. When you're full, walk around the grounds to see the new wave in farming oysters.

CoCoMo's

1134 Timberneck Road
Deltaville, VA 23043
804-776-8822

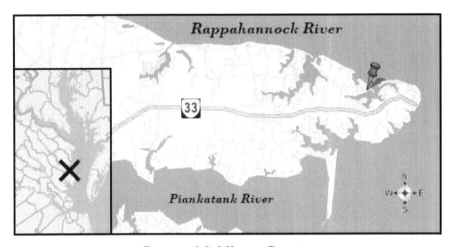

County: Middlesex County
Open: Seasonal; from Thursday to Sunday
Latitude: N 37° 33' 36" ⚓ Longitude: W 76° 19' 1"
Body of Water: Broad Creek off the Rappahannock River
Dockage: Yes
Driving Distance: Richmond: 70 miles,
Norfolk: 71 miles, Washington, DC: 139 miles

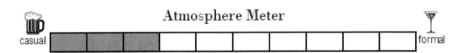

Atmosphere Meter

casual | | | | | | | | | | | formal

Palm trees appear along the Bay when you least expect it. But the tall one standing next to CoCoMo's seems to fit in perfectly with the restaurant's thatched umbrellas, tiki torches, and salmon pink and lime green walls. You almost feel like you've been swept way to the islands when you sip a signature cocktail, like the Cocomojito or Key West Cocktail, on the deck overlooking Broad Creek. When bands play on weekends, Deltaville turns into Margaritaville.

The octagonal building's indoor bar and dining areas are dressed up in their best tiki regalia. Walls are a colorful gallery of pressed tin, bright Caribbean hues, palm trees, and bamboo. Overhead fans made of wooden oars chase away the sticky summer heat.

To start your meal, you can go with traditional Chesapeake crab dip or pursue more tropical flavors with coconut shrimp. Fried seafood platters turn local oysters, scallops, and shrimp into crispy treats, but grilled tuna with pineapple curry sauce takes you one step closer to the islands. Meat favorites include cheesy chicken cordon bleu and filet mignon drizzled with a mushroom burgundy sauce. Want something lighter? Fresh salads, burgers, BLT sandwiches, or pulled pork BBQ should do the trick.

While gazing down at the marina, you might wonder about the floating homes with satellite dishes. They're called Aqua Lodges, which combine the cozy feel of a cottage with the mobility of a houseboat. They might be a fun way to complete your escape to island living.

Sandpiper Reef Restaurant

342 Misty Cove Road
Hallieford, VA 23068
804-725-3331
www.sandpiperreef.net

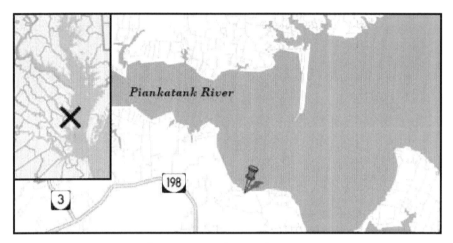

County: Mathews County
Open: Year Round
Latitude: N 37° 30' 11" ⚓ Longitude: W 76° 21' 2"
Body of Water: Godfrey Bay off the Piankatank River
Dockage: No
Driving Distance: Richmond: 68 miles,
Norfolk: 63 miles, Washington, DC: 142 miles

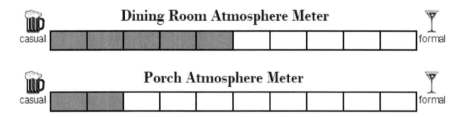

You might not get a panoramic waterfront view at
Sandpiper Reef, but you can order a dozen first-rate steamed
crabs and pick your fill on a lovely screened-in porch.

No bugs. No annoying seagulls trying to steal your hush puppies. Just you, a mallet, and 12 red hot beauties.

The Piankatank River is off in the distance, but the grove of tall pine trees provides shelter from summer heat and harsh winter winds. Plus the foosball table in the corner of the porch keeps youngsters occupied while adults finish their meal or catch up on the latest news.

Inside, the long dining room is broken into smaller intimate spaces by waist-high dividers. The ceiling is painted sky-blue, and pictures in black frames hang on cream-colored walls. The ambience is pleasant and comfortable.

Before ordering, check the weekly specials. That's where the kitchen shows off its skills with fresh seasonal ingredients. Soft-shell crunches in the spring yield to crispy fried oysters in the fall. All year round you'll enjoy the Nauti Pasta's blend of shrimp and scallops in a light garlic sauce or the seafood sampler where everybody jumps in the pool. Reef and Beef Kabobs present treasures from the sea and the land over a bed of grilled vegetables. Succulent Delmonico steaks are grilled just the way you like, and BBQ ribs are slow-cooked in a special house sauce. Blue ribbon desserts: pecan fudge pie and blueberry bread pudding.

Seabreeze Restaurant

34 Old Ferry Road
Grimstead, VA 23064
804-725-4000

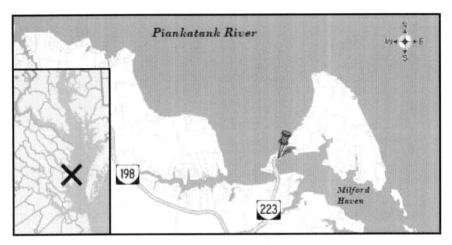

County: Mathews County
Open: Year Round
Latitude: N 37° 29' 33" ⚓ Longitude: W 76° 18' 35"
Body of Water: Milford Haven
Dockage: Yes
Driving Distance: Richmond: 71 miles,
Norfolk: 65 miles, Washington, DC: 146 miles

Atmosphere Meter

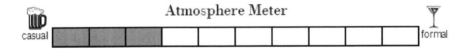

Seabreeze might be a petite restaurant on an island that's only four miles long, but it's got big beautiful scenery that makes this destination special. Tall loblolly pine trees cast shade on golden marshlands, and the panoramic view is expansive. A menagerie of different watercraft navigates the clear blue waters around you. It's seaside charm at its best.

Oyster tongs are mounted on the dining room wall above curtains made with blue and white lighthouse fabric. The restaurant and island are dry, but you can't beat the prices at this home-style crab house. Fresh fried soft-shells and crab cakes are simply delicious. Flounder, shrimp, and scallops are full of flavor. Fried chicken, liver with onions, and country fried steak show meat eaters that they left behind the world of calorie counters and entered a place filled with rich, savory pleasures.

Not far from Seabreeze is the Gwynn Island Museum with exhibits about local watermen, maritime traditions, war heroes, Indian artifacts, colonial relics, and vintage dresses. You can soak up local history and folklore, including the story about how Gwynn Island got its name.

According to legend, around 1611 an explorer named Hugh Gwynn was sailing where the Piankatank River meets the Bay. When he heard cries from an Indian girl who had fallen from her canoe, Gwynn dived into the water and pulled her to safety. This grateful but dripping wet gal was Pocahontas, daughter of the great Indian chief Powhatan. In appreciation for saving her life, the princess gave Gwynn the island where you just enjoyed a delightful meal.

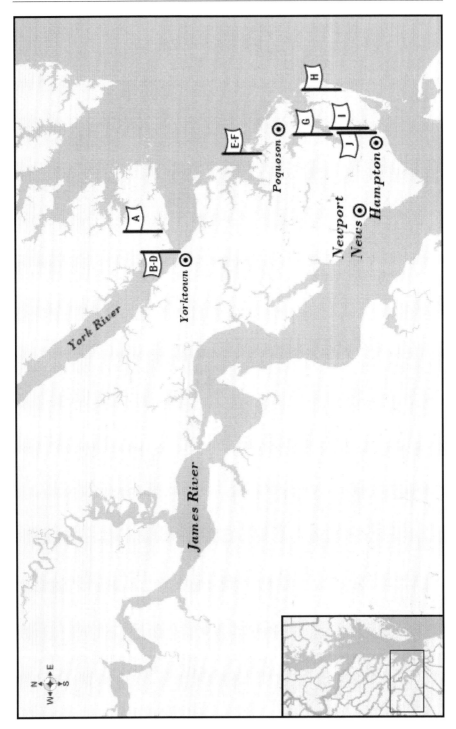

York River and Hampton

River's Inn Restaurant
& Crab Deck

8109 Yacht Haven Road
Gloucester Point, VA 23062
804-642-9942
www.riversinnrestaurant.com

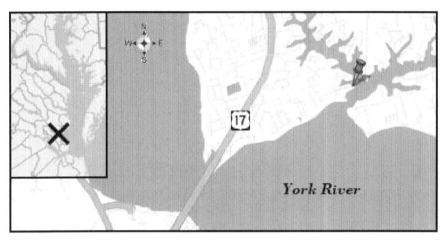

County: Gloucester County
Open: Year Round
Latitude: N 37° 15' 24" ⚓ Longitude: W 76° 28' 45"
Body of Water: Sarah Creek off the York River
Dockage: Yes
Driving Distance: Richmond: 66 miles,
Norfolk: 38 miles, Washington, DC: 167 miles

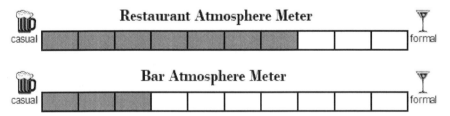

A gorgeous location wasn't enough for River's Inn. The owners envisioned more, so they built a restaurant where every seat in the house feels like the best place to be. If dining alfresco is your game, head out to the wooden deck and let the water wash away your worries. Take a seat on a captain's chair at the deck bar and investigate the whimsical artwork of crabs made from old car mufflers and a boat hung from the rafters. Acoustic bands play on weekends, and the atmosphere is fun and upbeat.

The inside dining areas' walls are painted in soothing earth tones and accented with gently lit nautical paintings. Tall windows afford a lovely waterfront view, and the fireplace casts a warm glow on cherry wood tables and chairs.

You might wonder if the food can meet the standards set by such a handsome place. The answer is a resounding yes. The chefs wow guests with culinary delights that marry Virginia and Louisiana cuisines with fresh local ingredients. Two styles of crab cakes vie for your attention: Chesapeake Classics with 4 ounces of jumbo lump meat or Bayou Classics served on fried green tomatoes with bronzed baby shrimp. York River oysters arrive daily to be eaten on the half shell or fried in po' boys. You can order chicken parmesan or marsala, or choose between hand-cut filet mignon or New York strip. Soups, breads, and sauces are all made from scratch in this ideal spot along Sarah Creek.

Riverwalk Restaurant
& High Tide Bar & Grill

323 Water Street
Yorktown, VA 23690
757-875-1522
www.riverwalkrestaurant.net

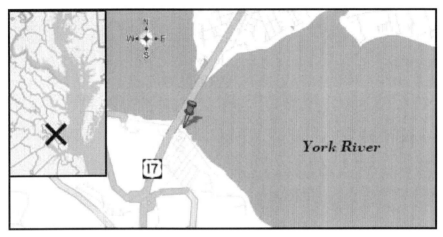

County: York County
Open: Riverwalk is year-round; High Tide is seasonal.
Latitude: N 37° 14' 20" ⚓ Longitude: W 76° 30' 31"
Body of Water: York River
Dockage: Yes
Driving Distance: Richmond: 62 miles,
Norfolk: 36 miles, Washington, DC: 164 miles

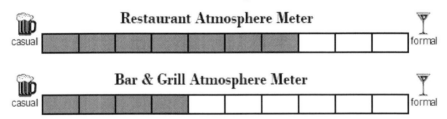

When Riverwalk opened in May 2005, Yorktown residents
breathed a sigh of relief. Since 1944, Nick's Seafood Pavilion

had claimed this spot, but the building was destroyed during Hurricane Isabel. The new restaurant was a sign of hope that the waterfront could be rebuilt. From the moment its doors opened, Riverwalk became the go-to place for fresh seafood.

A fountain bubbles out front, and the back faces a gorgeous view of Coleman Bridge spanning the York River. It's a sprawling place, and each dining area seems lovelier than the next. The menu is packed with innovative and traditional seafood dishes ranging from mojito shrimp cocktail to a Blue Plate Special (crab imperial, fried oysters, and saltine-crusted shrimp). The quarter-pound crab cake feels like a dare, and the Waterman's Pot Pie is the ultimate comfort food. Beef, lamb, and chicken are all-natural and organic.

High Tide Bar offers casual fare on the covered patio with burgers, sandwiches, salads, locally grown oysters, and ribs. The beer list is extensive, and Skinny Drinks blended with Crystal Light offer guilt-free pleasure with only 150 calories. After your meal, be sure to explore this charming area. Take a Segway tour of historic sites, check out the gift shops, visit the watermen's museum, or take a stroll on the beach.

The River Room Restaurant & the Island Café

508 Water Street
Yorktown, VA 23690
757-898-5270
www.dukeofyorkmotel.com

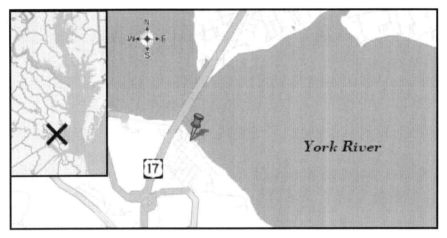

County: York County
Open: Year Round
Latitude: N 37° 14' 13" Longitude: W 76° 30' 26"
Body of Water: York River
Dockage: No
Driving Distance: Richmond: 62 miles,
Norfolk: 36 miles, Washington, DC: 164 miles

Atmosphere Meter

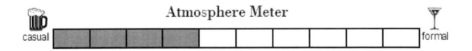

casual — formal

The River Room Restaurant and Island Café are tucked inside the Duke of York Hotel, which has a retro 1960s feel and a location that's hard to beat. The restaurants do not have an outdoor deck, but right outside you can stroll along the York River's sandy beach or take a trolley into town to visit the historic sites and quaint shops of Yorktown.

If you're an early riser, Island Café is the place to go for a good cup of Joe and specialty omelets filled with just about anything that suits your fancy. Lunch is also served here. Favorites include crab cakes, she-crab soup, sandwich wraps, and fried catch of the day.

The recently renovated River Room is the dinner destination. Tables are covered with white linens, but the atmosphere remains comfortable. The menu marries traditional American with Greek and Mediterranean cuisine. Your best bet: Order seafood, especially crab cakes, flounder, or shish kabobs that skewer lobster, shrimp, and scallops with tomato, onions, and mushrooms. Steaks, burgers, and sandwiches are tasty and filling. The kids' menu accommodates picky palates with the standard fare of pizza, chicken nuggets, and spaghetti.

Homemade desserts are legendary. Be sure to leave room in your belly for Baked Alaska, baklava, or coconut cream pie.

Yorktown Pub

540 Water Street
Yorktown, VA 23690
757-886-9964
www.yorktownpub.com

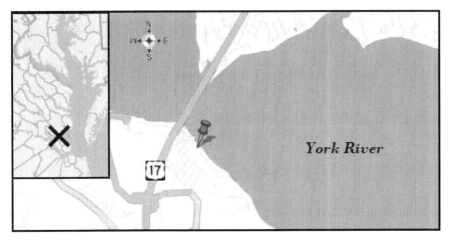

County: York County
Open: Year Round
Latitude: N 37° 14' 11" ⚓ Longitude: W 76° 30' 23"
Body of Water: York River
Dockage: No
Driving Distance: Richmond: 62 miles,
Norfolk: 36 miles, Washington, DC: 164 miles

Atmosphere Meter

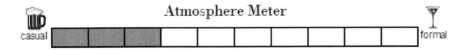

When you walk inside Yorktown Pub, you instantly feel right at home. Maybe it's the welcoming staff. Perhaps it's the smoky aroma of the wood burning fireplace. Or it could be that special feel of an old tavern where friends have gathered for decades. In 1951, the original owners called this place Gus's. In 1987, the current proprietors turned the building into a comfy, waterfront pub with knotty pine walls, booths with dark green leather seats, a long wooden bar with a smooth brass railing, and nautical items as décor.

Some taverns focus more on frosty mugs than food — but that's not the case here. A recent shift toward locally grown ingredients has created surprisingly tasty dishes. Buttery York oysters are plucked from the river nearby, scallops are delivered fresh from Seaford, VA, and the ahi tuna was caught off the Outer Banks. Soft-shell crabs are fried to a golden brown, and Shirley's seafood gumbo is packed with treasures from the local waters. Just follow the fresh catch board near the door, and you can't go wrong.

Also on the menu are treats for meat eaters: burgers, jerk chicken, nachos, BBQ pork on a bun, and sandwiches piled high with Boar's Head deli slices. Desserts are made in-house.

To enjoy Yorktown attractions, you can take sunset cruises that include dinner from the pub's kitchen. Or you can hike up the hill to see the battlefield where George Washington and his French allies forced England's Cornwallis to surrender in 1781 and bring an end to the American Revolution.

Owen's Marina Restaurant

259 Mingee Street
Poquoson, VA 23662
757-868-8407

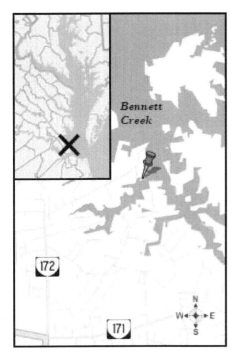

County: Poquoson (city)

Open: Seasonal

Latitude: N 37° 8' 46"

Longitude: W 76° 22' 28"

Body of Water: White House
Cove off Bennett Creek off the
Chesapeake Bay

Dockage: Yes

Driving Distance:
Richmond: 74 miles
Norfolk: 27 miles
Washington, DC: 175 miles

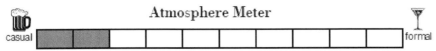

Atmosphere Meter

casual | | | | | | | | | | formal

The weather-worn sign with a blue crab, little-neck clams, and melted butter says it all — Owens Marina Restaurant showcases local seafood that watermen bring to its kitchen. While waiting to pick your fill of steamed crabs, kick back on the old wooden deck and watch boats chug by. Or check out the picker's paradise of stuff that washed ashore over the years and is stashed around the place. Everything from old boat motors to fishing gear, duck decoys, vintage captain statues, and a life-size plastic deer is on display.

The dining room has a homey, timeless feel with dark knotty pine walls, old photos, and hand-sewn curtains made of coffee cup printed fabric. Waitresses greet you warmly as if you were family. It's best to consult them before ordering, because they know what came in that day. If they suggest local crabs, clams, rockfish, or shrimp, don't hesitate to get them. Juicy burgers and sandwiches are also fine.

Nearby is the quaint town of Poquoson, which moves at a gentler pace than the bustling ports to its south. The name "Poquoson" is derived from the Algonquin Indian word for "great marsh," a prominent land feature in the area. Stroll through Poquoson's timeless streets or stop at the museum that celebrates its local maritime heritage and has a new Marsh Walk that takes you through the scenic breeding ground of the seafood you just ate.

Surf Rider Poquoson

1 Rens Road
Poquoson, VA 23662
757-868-0080

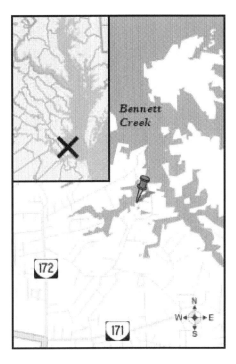

County: Poquoson (city)

Open: Year Round

Latitude: N 37° 8' 31"

Longitude: W 76° 22' 37"

Body of Water: White House
Cove off Bennett Creek off the
Chesapeake Bay

Dockage: Yes

Driving Distance:
Richmond: 73 miles
Norfolk: 26 miles
Washington, DC: 175 miles

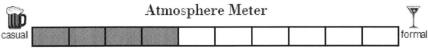

Atmosphere Meter

casual | | | | | | | | | | formal

In spring 2012, the Surf Rider Group introduced the latest addition to its family of restaurants to folks at the Poquoson Marina. The sound of hammers and saws fills the air, as developers expand the community with new seaside homes and additional slips and amenities for boaters.

Nestled in a tree-lined cove, the spacious building sits right on the water's edge, providing a front-row seat to Chesapeake wildlife and watercraft jaunting in and out of the marina. Sunset views are dazzling.

On the deck, live bands play under the stars on weekends. In the kitchen cooks crank out seafood caught right off shore. The house specialty crab cakes combine Old Bay, jumbo lump meat, and only a pinch of filler. Steamed shrimp and sautéed scallops taste delicious, and carnivores get goose bumps over the pulled pork BBQ and savory steaks.

While you nibble on seafood and soak up the view, try to imagine what this area was like 350 years ago. Algonquian Indians ruled this territory, and Powhatan was their famous chief, who forged a mighty coalition of 30 different tribes. They fished these waters and hunted game in the woodlands. Just think — Powhatan's daughter Pocahontas probably ate crabs on the same spot where you're dining today.

Checkered Flag Tavern

1721 North King Street
Hampton, VA 23669
757-723-3283

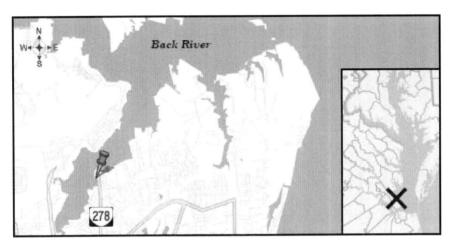

County: Hampton (city)
Open: Year Round
Latitude: N 37° 3' 55" ⚓ Longitude: W 76° 20' 55"
Body of Water: Southwest Branch of the Back River
Dockage: No
Driving Distance: Richmond: 78 miles,
Norfolk: 19 miles, Washington, DC: 179 miles

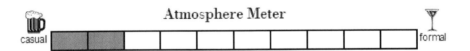

You can belly up to the bar and get an early afternoon beer buzz or shoot a game of pool with friends at this lively local watering hole. Pickup trucks parked out front of the Checkered Flag Tavern let you know that t-shirts and jeans are the preferred attire, and the atmosphere is casual.

The walls of the bar's indoor smoking area are covered with NASCAR posters, Budweiser signs, and big-screen TVs for watching sports events. Wednesday night pool tournaments attract local sharks, and bands on weekends crank out classic rock or country tunes. Karaoke evenings lure singers of all talent levels to the mic once they've got a few cocktails under their belt.

The outdoor deck is painted burgundy and gold, with a row of white lights strung across the top. The view of the water is slightly obscured by a row of tall pine trees, but the breeze off Back River cools you down on hot summer nights.

Food is standard pub fare — nothing fancy and generally well cooked. Jumbo shrimp, crab cakes, and fried oyster specials are delicious. Big juicy burgers and BBQ rib platters require extra napkins. And don't even bother to count calories if you order bacon cheddar fries, nachos, or Polish kielbasa with sauerkraut — just savor the flavor.

It's all about good times, rock and roll, and taking it easy when you hang out in this neighborhood favorite.

Water's Edge Bar & Grill
at Salt Ponds

11 Ivory Gull Crescent
Hampton, VA 23664
757-864-0336
www.saltpondsmarinaresort.com

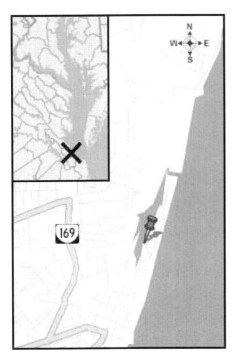

County: Hampton (city)

Open: Year Round

Latitude: N 37° 3' 13"

Longitude: W 76° 17' 13"

Body of Water: Salt Ponds off
the Chesapeake Bay

Dockage: Yes

Driving Distance:
Richmond: 81 miles
Norfolk: 19 miles
Washington, DC: 182 miles

Atmosphere Meter

casual   formal

Water's Edge is located at the largest marina on the lower Chesapeake Bay with 254 state-of-the-art floating slips and dockage for boats up to 110 feet. The building looks like a screw-pile lighthouse and feels like a beacon of merriment. Its wrap-around deck offers a fabulous waterfront view of boats cruising up the Bay or out to the Atlantic Ocean. Sport fishing in this area is legendary.

The restaurant's interior is easy on the eye, with deep rose-colored walls and a tongue-and-groove wooden skylight that lifts your gaze up to the heavens. Oars with boat names mounted around the bar lend a charming personal touch.

Down below on the ground level await a cabana bar and swimming pool that attract tiki fans seeking rum drinks and Polynesian-style relief from the summer heat.

The menu presents a nice array of dining options. You can start with crab dip, calamari, or cream of crab soup, or pick a skewer of beef, chicken, shrimp, or tuna. Sandwiches, wraps, and po' boys are hearty and accompanied by crispy French fries or crunchy hush puppies. Fish lovers can sink their teeth into a tender crab cake or dive into a medley of fresh catch on the seafood platter. And meat eaters won't leave hungry after they've taken the last bite of a thick-cut steak, sautéed chicken breast, or fist-sized burger.

Regatta Grille & Oyster Alley

700 Settlers Landing Road
Hampton, VA 23669
757-727-9700
www.hamptonmarinahotel.com/
hampton-marina-dining.html

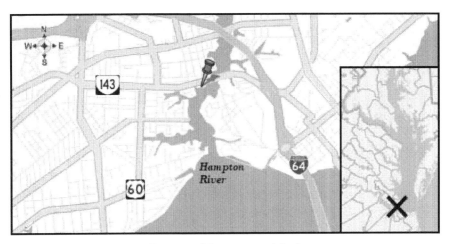

County: Hampton (city)
Open: Regatta, year round; Oyster Alley, seasonal
Latitude: N 37° 1' 28" ⚓ Longitude: W 76° 20' 31"
Body of Water: Hampton River
Dockage: Yes
Driving Distance: Richmond: 78 miles,
Norfolk: 16 miles, Washington, DC: 179 miles

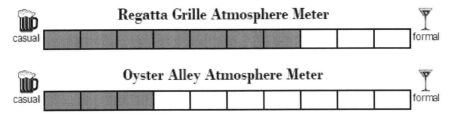

At Regatta, you won't leave your slip or parking space
until it's time to go home, because nearby attractions are in

walking distance. At Hampton History Museum, you learn about the city's 1610 beginnings and how it was burned to the ground in the Revolutionary and Civil Wars. You can take a cruise on the *Miss Hampton II*, tour the Virginia Air & Space Center, or visit Carousel Park's 200 antique merry-go-rounds.

After you work up a hearty appetite, head for Regatta where boats are docked so close to your table that you can almost reach out and touch them. Located in the Crowne Plaza Hotel, it's an inviting space decorated with trophies and photos of sailboat races.

Seafood is delivered daily by local watermen. Specialties include Cajun tuna bites, Atlantic salmon, Maryland crab cakes, shrimp and sausage grits, and pan-seared grouper. Salads, club sandwiches, burgers, and steaks round out the menu.

Take off your tie at Oyster Alley. This outdoor deck's atmosphere is much more relaxed along the water. Fresh oysters are presented four ways: Rockefeller, grilled, fried, or raw. The novelty Crab Sickles come on a stick and are dusted with Old Bay seasoning. The bun is smaller than the catch on the Huge Fish Sandwich, and deep-fried pickles make your lips pucker from its savory/tart competition. Sirloin burgers, chicken wings, and turkey wraps are favorites among meat eaters.

Surf Rider
Restaurant Bluewater

1 Marina Road
Hampton, VA 23669
757-723-9366

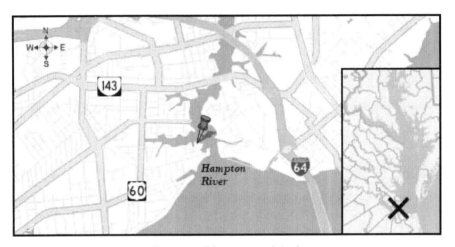

County: Hampton (city)
Open: Year Round
Latitude: N 37° 1' 1" ⚓ Longitude: W 76° 20' 35"
Body of Water: Hampton River
Dockage: Yes
Driving Distance: Richmond: 77 miles,
Norfolk: 19 miles, Washington, DC: 178 miles

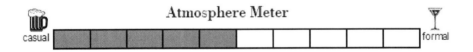

Surf Rider Bluewater is located in an area that changed
the course of U.S. history. During the Civil War, slaves
flocked to this area, because they were protected by Union

---

forces at Fort Monroe, who refused to return them to their Confederate masters. By the end of the war, about 10,000 slaves had migrated here, built homes, schools, and churches. They formed the Grand Contraband Camp, which was the first self-contained African American community. At the camp in 1863, the first reading in the South of the Emancipation Proclamation took place under an old oak tree that still grows on the campus of Hampton University. So, as you gaze across Surf Rider Bluewater's marina, raise a glass to a place that incubated American freedom.

Surf Rider Group owns five eateries in the Hampton Roads area, yet each one captures the feel of a lively neighborhood gathering place. The atmosphere at this location is upbeat casual, and the waterfront view is lovely.

Crab cakes are light on filler and heavy on jumbo lump meat, and crab pots offer a filling medley of local seafood. Rockfish, flounder, and shrimp are well-prepared and accompanied by crispy hush puppies. Meat lovers can take their pick of steaks, burgers, or chicken. And the famous key lime pie is the perfect ending to a hearty meal.

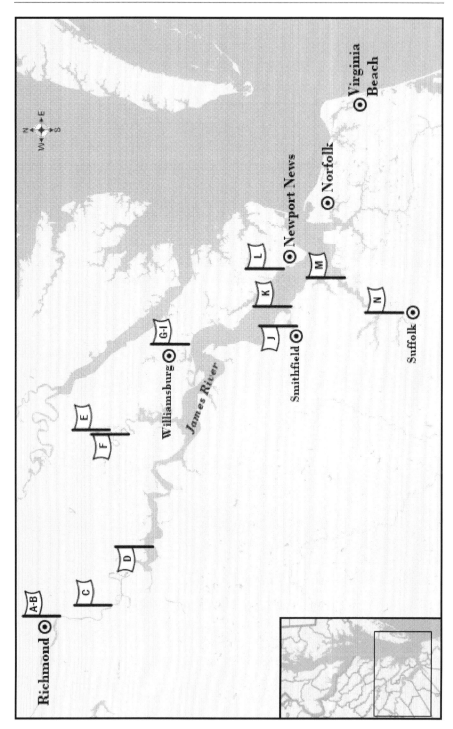

James River

The Boathouse Restaurant
at Rocketts Landing

4708 East Old Main Street
Richmond, VA 23231
804-622-2628
www.boathouserichmond.com

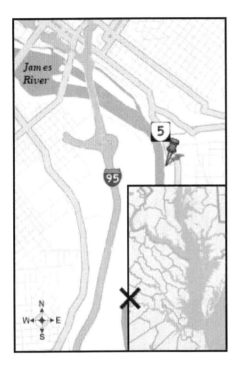

County: Richmond (city)

Open: Year Round

Latitude: N 37° 31' 5"

Longitude: W 77° 24' 57"

Body of Water: James River

Dockage: Yes

Driving Distance:
  Fredericksburg: 61 miles
  Norfolk: 92 miles
  Washington, DC: 109 miles

Atmosphere Meter

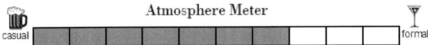

casual — formal

The stunning views of the James River and urban skyline from the Boathouse's twin decks make you wish Richmond had more waterfront dining spots. This strikingly beautiful restaurant is located on the edge of the city limits in the restored Power Plant building that used to generate electricity for trolley cars. The upscale décor is sophisticated and open, marrying steel, glass, and brick with watery blue and green tones. On the ceiling, wave-shaped metal light fixtures echo the flowing river below.

The food is harvested locally and environmentally kind, and the award-winning wine list accommodates every dish. A lobster tank near the entrance sends a message that seafood takes center stage here. Oysters come from the Piankatank River, tender hush puppies are filled with local crab, and mussels are bathed in a garlic and white wine broth. Entrée standouts: shrimp and grits with sausage and tomatoes, fried Chesapeake crab cakes, and seared scallop salad with goat cheese and toasted pumpkin seeds.

The wood stone oven lures you into ordering pizza with toppings such as crab and brie, or lamb sausage and cauliflower. Meat eaters get their fill of juicy steaks, lamb chops, and roasted chicken breast. When you pay your check, you'll be pleased to know that a percentage of sales supports environmental groups like Friends of the James River Park and Chesapeake Bay Foundation.

Conch Republic Rocketts

11 Orleans Street
Richmond, VA 23231
804-226-6242
www.conchrepublicrocketts.com

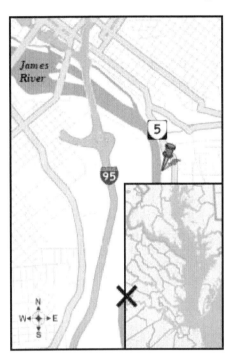

County: Richmond (city)

Open: Year Round

Latitude: N 37° 31' 3"

Longitude: W 77° 24' 57"

Body of Water: James River

Dockage: Yes

Driving Distance:
  Fredericksburg: 61 miles
  Norfolk: 92 miles
  Washington, DC: 109 miles

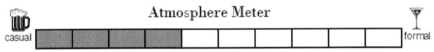

Atmosphere Meter

casual   formal

Want to enjoy a touch of Key West without the cost of airfare? Then head over to Conch Republic in Rocketts Landing, where they promise to help you "change your attitude without changing your latitude." Sipping a mai-tai at the thatched-roof and bamboo tiki bar is a perfect way to get your Jimmy Buffett groove going. Or you can kick back on the wrap-around deck, relish the terrific James River view, and listen to a band play under the stars. It's a laid-back locale designed for sweet summer evenings with friends.

The menu is island-inspired and Cajun influenced. Adventurous diners start with alligator bites or conch fritters. The shrimp dip with pita is creamy bliss. You can order a cheeseburger in this paradise, but seafood steals the show. Crab cakes and flounder po' boys come with lime tartar sauce, and jalapeno-mango sauce gives a kick to fresh grouper. Islamorada fish tacos with creamy chipotle sauce and pulled pork with guava BBQ are heavenly treats.

You might wonder about the restaurant's unusual name. In 1982, citizens of the Florida Keys were ticked off about a Border Patrol blockade on the only road leading to the U.S. mainland. Key West's mayor seceded from the United States and declared the Conch Republic an independent nation by breaking a piece of stale Cuban bread over the head of a man dressed in a Navy uniform. After one minute of rebellion, they surrendered and demanded $1 billion in foreign aid and war relief. Three cheers to their feisty spirit!

The Lily Pad Café

9680 Osborne Turnpike
Henrico, VA 23231
804-795-4155

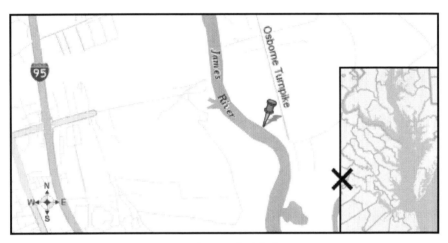

County: Chesterfield County
Open: Seasonal
Latitude: N 37° 24' 3" ⚓ Longitude: W 77° 23' 5"
Body of Water: James River
Dockage: Yes
Driving Distance: Richmond: 11 miles,
Norfolk: 94 miles, Washington, DC: 124 miles

Atmosphere Meter

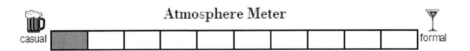

casual　　　　　　　　　　　　　　　　　　　formal

On a lazy summer afternoon, it's easy to while away the
hours at Lily Pad Café. It's rustic bliss, and everyone is
welcomed warmly at this dockside watering hole. Boats and
jet skis buzz around the marina, and the James River is right at
your fingertips. The one-story cinderblock building is painted

sky blue with green lily pads and pink shutters. A few potted tropical plants mark the outside patio area, and ceramic frogs squat on the tables. The best seats in the house are the wooden gliders with green canopies that help folks get respite from the sun. Just grab a plastic bucket of iced beer and hop inside.

If stormy weather chases you indoors, you'll find a small bar and dining room painted in cheerful blue and yellow. Bamboo trees and jumping frogs drawn on the walls give the space a little tiki touch.

Since it opened in 2003, printed menus haven't seemed necessary, because food choices change daily depending on what's in season. A chalkboard hung above the bar presents the options for your meal.

Seafood delivered fresh from local watermen is your best bet. Spicy fish tacos, hot steamed shrimp, and tender crab clusters are among the favorites. Egg salad with bacon is a creamy retro treat, and chicken quesadillas are always crowd pleasers. Juicy hamburgers and BBQ ribs round out the choices for meat lovers. It's generally simple home-made fare served with no frills and no hassles, at a place that knows how to kick back and celebrate the joys of summer.

Dockside Restaurant
& Schooner's Lounge

700 Jordan Point Road
Hopewell, VA 23860
804-541-2600
www.docksideonthejames.com

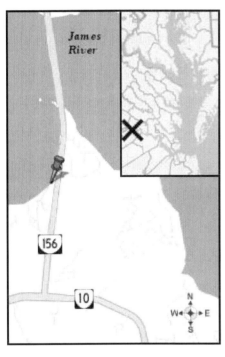

County: Prince George County

Open: Year Round

Latitude: N 37° 18' 13"

Longitude: W 77° 13' 26"

Body of Water: James River

Dockage: No

Driving Distance:
  Richmond: 23 miles
  Norfolk: 73 miles
  Washington, DC: 132 miles

Atmosphere Meter

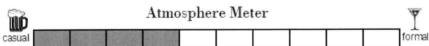

casual | | | | | | | | | | formal

When a recent storm blew out Dockside's dock, the staff didn't let the incident dampen their spirits. It's part of life along the water. They got to work rebuilding and serving good local seafood at a place that accepts the rivah in good times and bad. The waterfront view from the wrap-around deck is stunning, and the red awning shelters guests from scorching summer sun. The building's nine picture windows make sure inside diners don't miss any of the action on the river. The skylight on top of the beamed cathedral ceiling lets in just enough light to savor the old knotty pine walls.

Seafood is the house specialty: Local oysters, scallops, clam strips, and flounder come fried or broiled. Lump crab cakes are grilled golden brown, and shrimp are steamed to a perfect pink. Chicken salad and club sandwiches taste home-made, and thick burgers come with fries. Desserts like Kentucky Pie and Snickers Blitz can satisfy any sweet tooth.

While you're eating a scrumptious meal, take note of the bridge spanning the James. This vertical-lift bridge is named after Benjamin Harrison V, a signer of the Declaration of Independence and Virginia governor who lived nearby at Berkeley Plantation. It's worth a visit to see the oldest three-story brick mansion in Virginia and learn a little local history. At this location in December 1619, English settlers celebrated the first Thanksgiving, and in 1621 the first bourbon whiskey was distilled by an Episcopal priest.

Colonial Harbor
Marina Restaurant

14910 Marina Road
Lanexa, VA 23089
804-966-5523
www.colonialharbor.com/restaurant.html

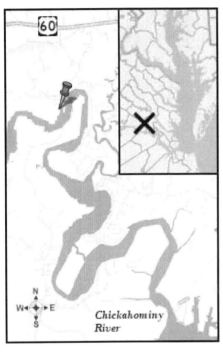

County: New Kent County

Open: Seasonal

Latitude: N 37° 24' 6"

Longitude: W 76° 54' 47"

Body of Water: Chickahominy
River off the James River

Dockage: Yes

Driving Distance:
Richmond: 35 miles
Norfolk: 63 miles
Washington, DC: 136 miles

Atmosphere Meter

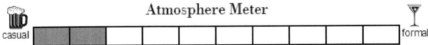

casual | | | | | | | | | | | formal

Down-home dining and a rollicking marina await you at
Colonial Harbor. At this low-key restaurant, you can eat in or
carry out, but staying put might be a better choice if you want
to get a glimpse of good times along the Chickahominy River.
White plastic patio furniture on the deck is shaded with big

red umbrellas that allow you to leisurely watch dogs chasing birds along the shore and neighbors chatting on their boats. Sunsets take your breath away.

Early birds can grab breakfast eggs with hash browns, grits, or biscuits. Sausage, bacon, and country ham are a local pride and joy. And a mountain of pancakes will keep you full well into the afternoon. The menu for the rest of the day features just-caught seafood: sautéed crab cakes, fried oysters or scallops, grilled tuna, and steamed shrimp. Tasty burgers, sizzling steaks, hot chicken wings, and BBQ pulled pork sandwiches are a carnivore's delight.

But keep in mind that the Chickahominy isn't just about feasts and fun in the sun. History is also part of the show. In 1607, Captain John Smith sailed up this 87-mile long river, hoping to reach the Pacific Ocean. He was captured by a band of Indian warriors and taken to Chief Powhatan. Not far from where you sit today, he was rescued by the chief's daughter, Pocahontas, who laid her head on Smith's head when her father raised a war club to execute the explorer.

The Blue Heron Restaurant

9100 Wilcox Neck Road
Charles City, VA 23030
804-829-9070
www.riversrest.com/facilities.htm

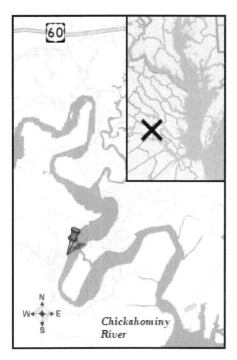

County: Charles City County

Open: Year Round

Latitude: N 37° 21' 47"

Longitude: W 76° 54' 45"

Body of Water: Chickahominy
River off the James River

Dockage: Yes

Driving Distance:
Richmond: 37 miles
Norfolk: 64 miles
Washington, DC: 138 miles

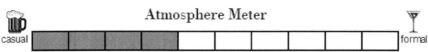

Atmosphere Meter

casual | | | | | | | | | | formal

All of your senses are activated when you come to the Blue Heron. Sure, the food gets your taste buds jumping, but take a moment before you settle into a meal and absorb all the other elements that make this place special. Listen to the children's laughter at the hotel pool next door or the band warming up for a gig. Watch fishermen haul heavy strings of the pickerel, yellow perch, catfish, or gar they caught that day. Feel the gentle breeze rolling up from the river, making everyone a bit more comfortable. And let your nose take in the briny river air combined with the kitchen aroma of seafood steamed in Old Bay.

After you slide across the brown leather cushion of a booth, investigate the daily specials. The fresh catch is a guaranteed good pick, especially when crabs and oysters are in season. Grilled tuna and shrimp from the steamer are wise choices any time of year.

Two Chef's Specials are quite tasty: Captain's Filet Mignon topped with a crab cake, shrimp, and drizzled with béarnaise sauce, and scallops stuffed with shrimp and capped with lump crabmeat. Burgers, po' boys, and country-style steak accommodate meat eaters' whims. And salads are made fresh with locally grown greens.

Three signature desserts are music to a sugar-lover's ears: Banana Foster Ice Cream Cake, Chocolate Confusion Cake (layers of chocolate cake, mousse, frosting, and chocolate chips), and Strawberry Shortcake with whipped cream. Yum!

Bray Dining Room

1010 Kingsmill Road
Williamsburg, VA 23185
757-253-1703
www.kingsmill.com/bray-bistro

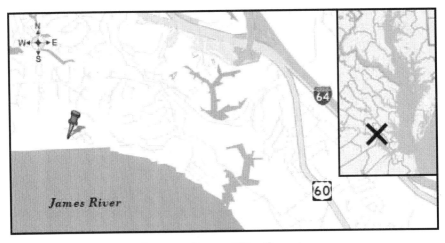

County: James City County
Open: Year Round
Latitude: N 37° 13' 29" ⚓ Longitude: W 76° 40' 2"
Body of Water: James River
Dockage: Yes
Driving Distance: Richmond: 56 miles,
Norfolk: 43 miles, Washington, DC: 158 miles

Atmosphere Meter

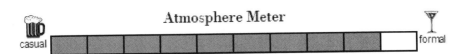

casual — formal

Next to Bray Dining Room four benches face each other in what appears to be a peaceful outdoor sitting area at the upscale Kingsmill Resort. Upon close inspection you realize that these benches mark the outline of the foundation for the main house and water well at the Bray Plantation. It was built around 1700 and spanned 1,300 acres of land along the James. The estate belonged to James Bray I, a heavy hitter in colonial politics: justice of the peace, member of the House of Burgesses, and alderman for the City of Williamsburg.

Lavish living awaits you inside this elegant hall that overlooks the James River. Crisp white linens and crystal bud vases cover the tables, black tapered chandeliers dangle gracefully overhead, and a grand piano lounges in the corner. Sliding doors lead out to a lovely deck with cast-iron and glass patio furniture.

The chefs built their menu around the idea of "sophisticated Southern cuisine," which gives favorite comfort foods a nouvelle twist with fresh local ingredients. Oyster po' boys and shrimp are dressed up in rémoulade sauce instead of Old Bay. Creamy corn and crab chowder is velvety smooth. Roast duck, thick-cut steaks, and portabella mushrooms filled with polenta are menu favorites. The popular Friday night seafood buffet presents a cornucopia of fresh catch, and Sunday brunch takes eggs, bacon, and toast to new epicurean heights.

If you're looking for a more casual venue during your visit, head over to Eagles, a golf-themed seafood and steak house a few steps away. Or walk up a flight of stairs to Moody's Tavern, a cozy lounge with a pool table, game boards, and chandeliers made of deer antlers.

Regattas'

1010 Kingsmill Road
Williamsburg, VA 23185
757-253-1703
www.kingsmill.com/regattas

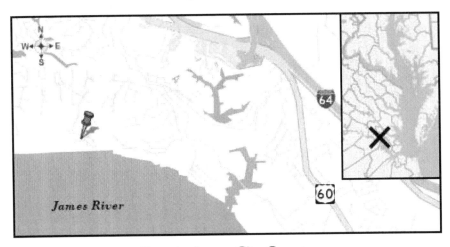

County: James City County
Open: Year Round
Latitude: N 37° 13' 29" ⚓ Longitude: W 76° 39' 56"
Body of Water: James River
Dockage: Yes
Driving Distance: Richmond: 56 miles,
Norfolk: 43 miles, Washington, DC: 158 miles

Atmosphere Meter

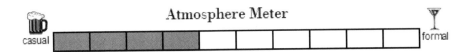

casual ————————————————————————— formal

Regattas' is just a stone's throw away from Williamsburg,
Jamestown, Busch Gardens, and other popular Virginia
attractions. And it's the casual dining alternative at
Kingsmill's luxury resort. The restaurant is surrounded with

amenities such as three championship golf courses, tennis courts, a spa and fitness center, and swimming pools.

Regattas' is only open for lunch and dinner, but it's a terrific place to feed your family and rest your weary feet after a long day of sightseeing. The small bar area is next to a gift shop, and an outdoor patio overlooks the James River.

Designers opted to give the dining room a bright contemporary feel. Colorful sailboat paintings, royal blue booths, and wooden chairs with red seat cushions create a vibrant vibe. Ivy hangs in planters from thick wooden rafters that run across the ceiling. Nautical items, such as an antique scuba helmet and hand-painted fish sculptures, underscore the casual ambience in this in this family-friendly spot.

Pizzas baked in a red tile, wood-burning stove come to your table with the cheese still bubbling. Crisp salads are big enough for two friends to share. Seafood dishes are caught in local waters and feature crabmeat, shrimp, oysters, and clams. Black Angus steaks and tender chicken breasts make sure meat eaters leave with a full belly.

James Landing Grille

1010 Kingsmill Road
Williamsburg, VA 23185
757-253-1703
www.kingsmill.com/jameslandinggrille

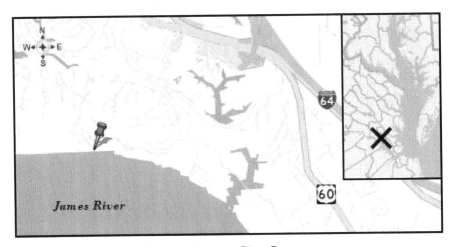

County: James City County
Open: Year Round
Latitude: N 37° 13' 23" ⚓ Longitude: W 76° 39' 47"
Body of Water: James River
Dockage: Yes
Driving Distance: Richmond: 56 miles,
Norfolk: 43 miles, Washington, DC: 158 miles

Atmosphere Meter

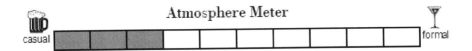

casual ▢▢▢▢▢▢▢▢▢▢▢ formal

Kingsmill Resort Marina had ambitious plans for 2012 — to build a brand new restaurant in time for the high summer season. Well, three cheers for the architects, electricians, and plumbers who met their deadlines so everyone could enjoy this waterfront gem right when the temperatures started to rise. But they're not quite finished working: Also on the facility's drawing board is a ship store with supplies, restrooms, showers, and jet ski rentals.

Now that the sawdust is swept away and everything's running smoothly, guests can grab a bite to eat or drink a cold one on the deck. The view is among the best along the James River, with boats tied up to the dock and children playing on the beach. Two levels of indoor dining space with spacious windows make sure everyone can witness spectacular sunsets.

The atmosphere is casual/nice, and the new menu takes advantage of the region's bounty of fresh seafood and produce. Appetizer standouts include fried oysters dipped in buttermilk and cornmeal, sautéed shrimp and grits, and two-salsa fish tacos with crème fraîche.

The grilled seafood trio entrée brings together scallops, shrimp, and Arctic char on top of vegetable risotto, and crab cakes come with fingerling potatoes. Summer succotash is an ideal swim buddy for pan-seared rockfish. Three meat dishes get a thumbs-up: charbroiled New York strip steak, grilled cilantro-lime chicken breast, and pork tenderloin cutlet.

The Restaurant at Smithfield Station

415 South Church Street
Smithfield, VA 23430
757-357-7700
www.smithfieldstation.com

County: Isle of Wight County
Open: Year Round
Latitude: N 36° 58' 56" ⚓ Longitude: W 76° 37' 21"
Body of Water: Pagan River off the James River
Dockage: Yes
Driving Distance: Richmond: 73 miles,
Norfolk: 26 miles, Washington, DC: 180 miles

Atmosphere Meter

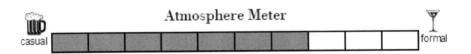

casual   formal

    It's easy to spend the day at Smithfield Station. In addition to a lovely family-run restaurant, you can enjoy the marina, hotel, and an adorable river port town that bustles with shops and is home to the world-famous Smithfield hams. Local attractions include Windsor Castle Park with canoeing and hiking trails, Isle of Wight County Museum with exhibits ranging from prehistoric fossils to edible pork products, and a restored courthouse dating back to 1750 when the city was established. Walking the streets among the quaint Victorian homes takes visitors back to a simpler way of living.

Next to Smithfield Station stands a lighthouse where you can spend the night above the water. Beautiful waterfront rooms with upscale amenities are also available at the lodge. The restaurant's building is grand, with wrap-around decks and architecture influenced by its turn-of-the-century neighbors. Warm amber-colored wood walls are decorated with nautical items and vintage photos of the region. Tables are covered with crisp white cloths, but the atmosphere is informal and comfortable.

The award-winning kitchen is known for fresh seafood, pork dishes, and Sunday brunch buffet. The house specialty crab cakes, coconut shrimp, and oysters Rockefeller come to your table with crunchy hush puppies. Of course, ham is a featured meat, but burgers, steaks, and chicken are players on the menu. And before you leave, give in to the temptation to buy a Smithfield ham. You'll be in hog heaven at the first bite.

Captain Chuck-A-Muck's Sandbar & Grill

21088 Marina Road
Rescue, VA 23424
757-356-1005
www.captainchuck-a-mucks.com

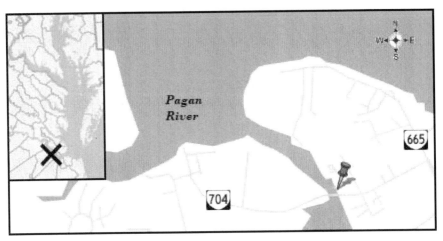

County: Isle of Wight County
Open: Year Round
Latitude: N 36° 59' 41" ⚓ Longitude: W 76° 33' 43"
Body of Water: Jones Creek off the Pagan River off the James River
Dockage: Yes
Driving Distance: Richmond: 78 miles,
Norfolk: 25 miles, Washington, DC: 186 miles

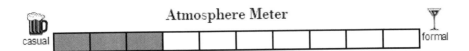

Having a bad day? Need something to cheer you up?
Then scoot over to Captain Chuck-A-Muck's. Heck, even the
name should make you smile. It's a happy place at a gorgeous

waterfront location that serves fresh, home-style food. Built in 1998 and then damaged by fire in 2002, this upbeat eatery is fully renovated and ready to roll.

The outside of the building is painted a simple gray with red trim, but metal buckets converted into light fixtures give the first clue that fun is a priority here. The knotty pine walls inside are decorated with everything from an American flag to trophy fish and a papier-mâché pig. Pepto-Bismol pink seats are lined up at the bar.

You'll see the Captain grilling crab cakes in the kitchen, racing around the dining room, and making sure everything's shipshape. This restaurant is a dream come true for him and his wife, so customer satisfaction reigns supreme.

Appetizer highlights are Tangy Tiki Bar Shrimp and Home-Made Unisex Crab Soup. The star of the entrees is the seafood sampler, piled high with crab, scallops, shrimp, and fish delivered each morning by local watermen. Angus steaks, burgers, and chicken take care of meat cravings. And desserts like key lime pie make you glad you came.

The Crab Shack
Seafood Restaurant

7601 River Road
Newport News, VA 23607
757-245-2722
www.crabshackonthejames.com

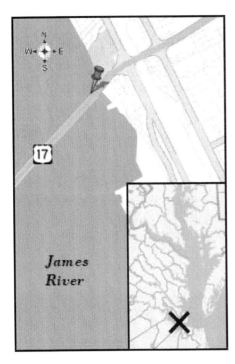

County: Newport News (city)

Open: Year Round

Latitude: N 37° 0' 48"

Longitude: W 76° 27' 23"

Body of Water: James River

Dockage: No

Driving Distance:
  Richmond: 73 miles
  Norfolk: 27 miles
  Washington, DC: 174 miles

Atmosphere Meter

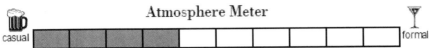

casual — formal

When a restaurant is located next door to a fishing pier, it's hard to think of anything but fresh seafood. And that's what happens at the Crab Shack. It started in 1993 as a seasonal outdoor deck at the foot of the expansive James River

Bridge. Renovations in 1997 created enclosed space for up to 200 hungry guests to sink their forks into the daily catch.

The atmosphere is comfortable and welcoming. Model boats and a stuffed blue marlin greet you at the door. Floor-to-ceiling windows framed in wood give everyone a front-row seat to spectacular sunsets on the water. A colorful fish mosaic and strings of starfish draped from the ceiling decorate the small bar in the back.

Burgers and chicken appear on the menu, but the main attraction is fresh seafood, with a staggering array of choices: local oysters fried or fresh from the raw bar, crabs cooked in soup or steamed and ready to pick, shrimp chilled for cocktails or dressed up in coconut batter, and flounder topped with béarnaise sauce. Can't pick just one? The seafood platter provides a sumptuous sampling of the kitchen's best.

If you haven't had your fill of the local waters, go out on the pier with the fishermen who drop lines into the water in pursuit of croaker, trout, or striped bass. Enjoy the parade of boats cruising under the bridge. Or head to Newport News, one of America's busiest harbors and shipyards since the 1700s. You'll discover a maritime museum, historic sites, and cultural attractions about the area's nautical heritage.

Bennett's Creek Restaurant

3305 Ferry Road
Suffolk, VA 23435
757-484-8700

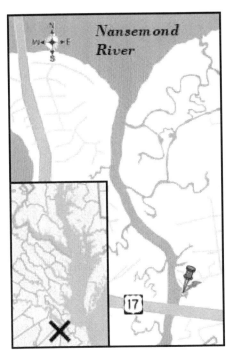

County: Suffolk (city)

Open: Year Round

Latitude: N 36° 51' 54"

Longitude: W 76° 28' 41"

Body of Water: Bennett's Creek
off the Nansemond River off
the James River

Dockage: Yes

Driving Distance:
Richmond: 90 miles
Norfolk: 13 miles
Washington, DC: 191 miles

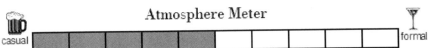

Atmosphere Meter

casual ... formal

Seeing only a plain white sign with the word "restaurant" perched on top of the building makes you wonder if you arrived at Bennett's Creek. But once you step inside this quaint little eatery, you know the trip to this hard-to-find location was worth it. This hidden jewel sits right on the water's edge at a lovely marina next to a bridge. The view from the outdoor deck is delightful, and weekends nights listening to live music washes your troubles away.

Flooding in 2011 caused some damage, but repairs are complete and the place looks shiny and new. The small bar area is cozy and packed with locals from the neighborhood. One wall is covered with watercolor paintings of tiki bars and palm trees. In the dining room, you can look at a mural of waterfowl soaring through a rosy sunset, or you could glance out the floor-to-ceiling windows to enjoy the real thing. Both are pleasantly soothing.

Try not to fill up on the warm hush puppies and bread basket, or you won't have room for local seafood dishes. The kitchen hits a home run with shrimp scampi and blackened tuna steak. Butterflied beef tenderloin stuffed with crabmeat and drizzled with béarnaise sauce is love at first bite, and crab cakes are crispy on the outside with tender lumps inside. Scallops, oysters, and calamari are just-caught fresh.

Constant's Wharf Grill

100 East Constance Road
Suffolk, VA 23434
757-925-1300
www.hiltongardeninnsuffolk.com

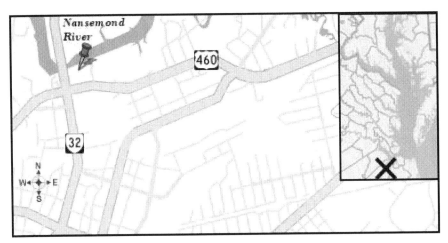

County: Suffolk (city)
Open: Year Round
Latitude: N 36° 44' 20" ⚓ Longitude: W 76° 34' 51"
Body of Water: Nansemond River off the James River
Dockage: Yes
Driving Distance: Richmond: 81 miles,
Norfolk: 19 miles, Washington, DC: 204 miles

Atmosphere Meter

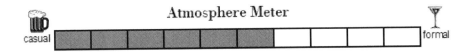

casual / formal

Tall white pillars give this big brick building a classic
Southern charm, and Constant's Wharf Grill follows suit with
a graceful dining experience. Located in the Hilton Garden
Inn, the covered brick patio overlooks a park and marina at

the Nansemond River. Parents spread out blankets for children to enjoy a summer concert on the lawn.

Boats slowly pull up at the docks, and rocking chairs next to the patio encourage lazy summer days with mint juleps in hand. An American flag flaps in the breeze next to brickwork designed to look like a compass.

Inside the dining area, staff serves breakfast, lunch, and dinner that will please all the guests. Local seafood, steaks, and chicken are well-prepared. Artisan woodwork on the bar cabinets shows an eye for detail, and big muted prints of wine labels add an interesting touch. Tall French doors bring in soft daylight, and wooden chairs with pastel green seat cushions are pushed under tables with matching cloth napkins.

After delivering a pair of plump crab cakes, a waitress explained how the restaurant got its name. According to local legend, John Constant was the area's first English settler and built the wharf around 1720. Thanks in part to him, Suffolk was a hub for trading tobacco, corn, gin, wine, and lumber. In the 1950s the city constructed a major road to alleviate traffic congestion, but accidentally misspelled his name. It was too costly to print new signs for Constance Road, so the founding father's name lives on in an awkward roadside typo.

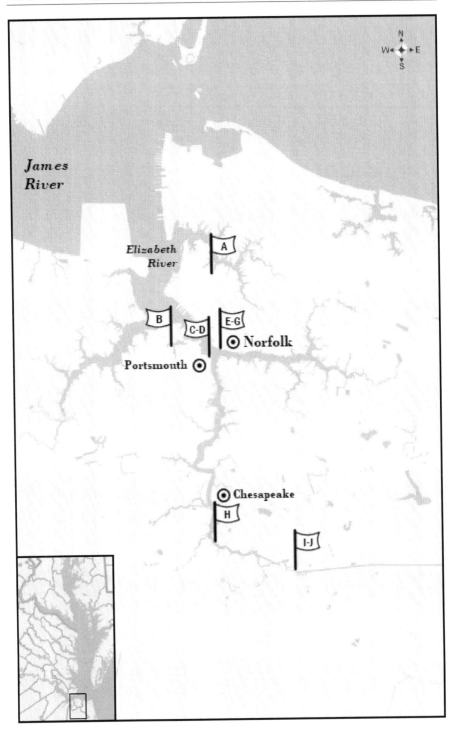

Elizabeth River

O'Sullivan's Wharf
Seafood Restaurant

4300 Colley Avenue
Norfolk, VA 23508
757-961-0899
www.osullivanswharf.com

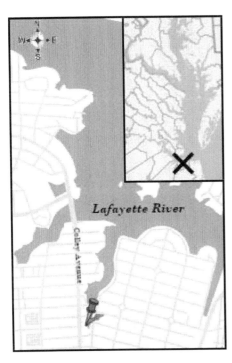

County: Norfolk (city)

Open: Year Round

Latitude: N 36° 53' 1"

Longitude: W 76° 17' 40"

Body of Water: Knitting Mill
Creek off the Lafayette River
off the Elizabeth River

Dockage: Yes

Driving Distance:
Richmond: 90 miles
Virginia Beach: 21 miles
Washington, DC: 191 miles

Atmosphere Meter

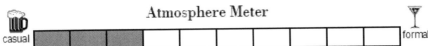

casual ─────────────────── formal

Happy hour at O'Sullivan's starts promptly at 3:00 p.m. and lasts over three hours. It's a rollicking neighborhood tavern where bands play on weekends, locals chuckle over pitchers of beer, and food comes out piping hot. The unassuming one-story building is painted white with blue trim, and the only nod to its Irish heritage is a tiny shamrock tucked inside the sign's letter "O."

The restaurant has a homey feel, with patrons bellied up to the bar placed in the middle of one dining area. An interior brick wall with twin arched openings leads to another eating space. Unfinished wooden tables on the back deck provide a waterfront view. Rustic fountains spray water to keep the current moving in the creek. It's not a sweeping panoramic view, but it is unique.

In the corner, a carved-wood statue of an Indian watches as waitresses patiently take orders for down-home cooking that mixes local seafood with hearty pub fare.

It's hard to resist the Old Bay Chips — thinly sliced deep-fried potatoes seasoned with the Chesapeake's favorite spice. The shrimp and clam chowder is velvety smooth, and char-grilled tuna bites are dusted with lemon pepper.

"The Steamer" is a virtual melting pot of crab legs, shrimp, clams, and oysters. "The Indecisive" marries the best of both worlds by serving large ocean shrimp with a hand-cut Delmonico steak. Burgers, chicken wraps, fresh salads, and deli meat sandwiches offer lighter fare that are best washed down with a rich brown stout.

The Flagship Restaurant

103 Constitution Avenue
Portsmouth, VA 23704
757-398-1600
www.flagshipportsmouth.blogspot.com

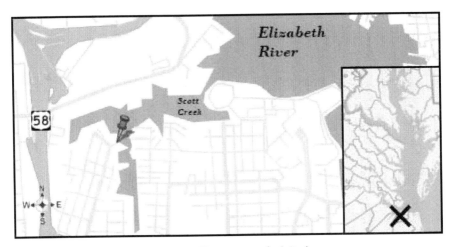

County: Portsmouth (city)
Open: Year Round
Latitude: N 36° 50' 40" ⚓ Longitude: W 76° 19' 21"
Body of Water: Scott Creek off the Elizabeth River
Dockage: Yes
Driving Distance: Richmond: 96 miles,
Norfolk: 4 miles, Washington, DC: 197 miles

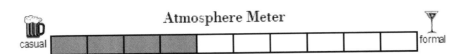

This hidden gem off the beaten path and is a lovely place to escape the urban bustle of Norfolk and Portsmouth. Tucked away in a marina, Flagship has a cozy atmosphere that makes you feel right at home the minute you arrive.

A blue awning covers the outdoor wooden deck, and a fireplace crackles in the corner when the temperature drops. On summer weekends, live acoustic guitar music brightens the mood, and sunsets along the water are a sight to behold.

At the bar, a fish imbedded in blue and green stained glass artwork eavesdrops on locals exchanging stories about their day. The dining area's round windows and gentle indirect lighting create an intimate ambience. The floor is covered with unique burnt orange and tan tile work.

The restaurant's garden provides fresh herbs and produce that follow the season's harvest. Other ingredients are bought from local watermen and farmer's markets. Mix it all together and you're guaranteed to eat healthy, flavorful food.

The signature dish, steamed shrimp, breaks from tradition by rejecting Old Bay. Instead, the cook uses butter, garlic, herbs, and white wine to create a sauce that requires toasted baguettes to soak up every drop. Crab cakes, tuna carpaccio, steamed mussels, and grilled rockfish are lip-smacking good. Savory meat specialties include baby back ribs, steak gorgonzola alfredo, and chicken marsala. It's all about the power of fresh simple cooking at a location that makes you want to linger for hours.

Half Shells Restaurant

10 Crawford Parkway
Portsmouth, VA 23704
757-398-1221

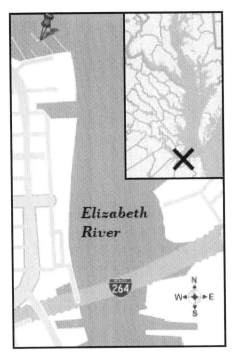

County: Portsmouth (city)

Open: Year Round

Latitude: N 36° 50' 29"

Longitude: W 76° 17' 53"

Body of Water: Elizabeth River

Dockage: Yes

Driving Distance:
Richmond: 97 miles
Norfolk: 3 miles
Washington, DC: 199 miles

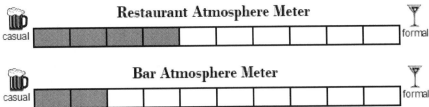

Sometimes in the crab deck scene, people like to make changes to keep a business fresh and current. That's why The Deck Restaurant switched its name to Half Shells in April 2012. It's still owned by the same welcoming family, and the view of Norfolk's city skyline is just as amazing as ever. They built a new tiki bar on the deck and started mixing cool blender drinks to chase away the summer heat. Now you can watch the boats cruise by while sipping on Rum Runners or frozen strawberry daiquiris. A lengthy martini list uses flavored vodkas to create specialty drinks such as the Marina Mama and Boat Rocker.

The second floor dining room has retained its clean, casual décor, and a revised menu introduces new dishes while keeping some of the old favorites. Local seafood still dominates entrée selections, with crab cakes, fried shrimp, and fish and chips leading the pack. But newcomers like Blue Point and Prince Island oysters are giving the other shellfish a run for their money. Beef tenderloin, New York strip steaks, pork osso bucco, and fried chicken are available for hungry meat eaters.

So, the next time you're in town swing by Half Shells, check out the new digs, and enjoy one of the most spectacular views in Norfolk Harbor.

Foggy Point Bar & Grill

425 Water Street
Portsmouth, VA 23704
757-673-3000

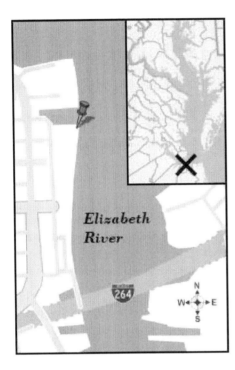

County: Portsmouth (city)

Open: Year Round

Latitude: N 36° 50' 17"

Longitude: W 76° 17' 45"

Body of Water: Elizabeth River

Dockage: No

Driving Distance:
  Richmond: 97 miles
  Norfolk: 3 miles
  Washington, DC: 198 miles

 Atmosphere Meter

casual ▮▮▮▮▮▮▮▮▮□□□ formal

Even though it's located in the Renaissance Hotel —
which can be a turn-off for some crab deck purists — Foggy
Bottom is a place worth visiting. It's handsome and spacious
with a casual contemporary feel. The waterfront brick patio
offers a great view of ships parading through Norfolk's busy
harbor. A tall fish tank at the entrance sends a message that

its loyalties lie with the sea. Intricate blue-and-white tile work on the bar echoes that sentiment. The floor-to-ceiling wall of windows makes sure everyone has a good view of the water.

The comfortable upscale dining room has smooth wood floors and soft beige walls decorated with pen-and-ink drawings of boat designs. Cushioned booths are clad in burgundy and cream fabric, and modern light fixtures bring a dash of color to the space.

The menu focuses on fresh local seafood. Crab, shrimp, scallops, and flounder get top billing. You can satisfy meat cravings with steaks, burgers, and chicken. The kitchen is open for breakfast, lunch, and dinner, which accommodates folks who want to explore local attractions. Lovely Old Towne Portsmouth, founded in 1752, is steeped in history, as well as specialty shops and antique stores. Also nearby you'll find sites to make the whole family happy: Children's Museum of Virginia, Nauticus National Maritime Center, Virginia Sports Hall of Fame, and Norfolk National Shipyard. It's a great area for a get-away.

Joe's Crab Shack

333 Waterside Drive
Norfolk, VA 23510
757-625-0655
www.joescrabshack.com

County: Norfolk (city)
Open: Year Round
Latitude: N 36° 50' 38"   Longitude: W 76° 17' 27"
Body of Water: Eastern Branch of the Elizabeth River
Dockage: No
Driving Distance: Richmond: 92 miles,
Virginia Beach: 18 miles, Washington, DC: 194 miles

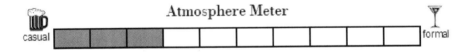

Joe's Crab Shack looks like a hoarder's paradise. You're surrounded by every imaginable nautical item from water skis to pelicans and boats. A super-sized plastic shark hovers above your table. The atmosphere is boisterous, and it's part of a Houston-based chain with 126 other locations. But there's something contagiously fun about this place. Maybe it's the location. The spacious eatery with a long covered deck is placed front and center on Norfolk's waterfront where ships of every shape and size cruise past your table. Perhaps it's the kids' play area that shows this restaurant understands parents' plight of entertaining restless children while waiting for meals to arrive.

Whatever the reason, people flock to Joe's for family-friendly eats. Eight types of steam pots, ranging from The Old Bay steamer to The Raging Cajun, are popular cauldrons of seafood representing various regional catches. Buckets of Crab are filled with spidery Dungeness legs, and Big Platters overflow with mounds of fried shrimp, fish, and clams. Shore to Please entrees include Skillet Paella, silky Crawfish Half & Half, and Shrimp Pasta Alfredo.

Meat eaters are not ignored on the menu, with items such as the 12-ounce rib eye steak or the cheesy fried chicken with creamy mushroom gravy. Bacon cheese burgers and chicken club sandwiches are tucked between toasted buns. The Sea Turtle Sundae and Chocolate Shack Attack are tasty sweets.

The City Dock Restaurant

777 Waterside Drive
Norfolk, VA 23510
757-622-2868
www.sheratonnorfolkwaterside.com/restaurant

County: Norfolk (city)
Open: Year Round
Latitude: N 36° 50' 38" Longitude: W 76° 17' 22"
Body of Water: Eastern Branch of the Elizabeth River
Dockage: No
Driving Distance: Richmond: 92 miles,
Virginia Beach: 18 miles, Washington, DC: 194 miles

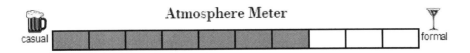

As you stroll along Norfolk's waterfront near City Dock Restaurant, you notice a series of plaques that commemorate local history. One explains the 300 years of ferry service at this bustling port and encourages you to take a paddle wheel taxi across to Portsmouth, if you're so inclined. Another tells how the Elizabeth River was named after Princess Elizabeth Stuart, daughter of England's King James I, who gave his name to the Jamestown Colony. A third marker spins the tale of when British Lord Dunsmore bombarded the town in 1776, because citizens refused to supply provisions for his ships.

When your historic walk is complete, stop at City Dock for refreshments. It's located in the Sheraton Hotel and occupies an open, airy space with a terrific waterfront view. Cobalt blue chairs and glasses pick up the aquatic hues from the river, and nautical prints hang upon the walls.

Seafood and regional favorites are served in a relaxed setting. Cooks think beyond traditional crab cakes by conjuring up creative dishes such as blue crab macaroni and cheese and creamy crab fondue. Eastern Shore fried oysters float in an Old Bay beurre blanc sauce, and seared rockfish is speckled with capers, black olives, and tomatoes. Pork tenderloin is stuffed with mushroom cornbread, and the fried chicken Caesar salad has a fresh resounding crunch.

Vintage Kitchen

999 Waterside Drive
Norfolk, VA 23510
757-625-3370
www.vintage-kitchen.com

County: Norfolk (city)
Open: Year Round
Latitude: N 36° 50' 35" ⚓ Longitude: W 76° 17' 16"
Body of Water: Eastern Branch of the Elizabeth River
Dockage: No
Driving Distance: Richmond: 92 miles,
Virginia Beach: 18 miles, Washington, DC: 194 miles

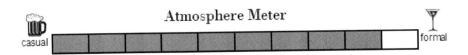

Virginia's second-largest city (behind Virginia Beach) needed a chic eatery on its revitalized waterfront, so Vintage Kitchen answered Norfolk's call. It's a sophisticated place with a ballroom, terrace, herb garden, and a stunning view of the Elizabeth River. By appointment or invitation only, guests are treated to an exclusive peek at the kitchen in action.

In the dining area, ivory walls, burled wood floors, black cushioned benches, and smooth white tables establish an elegant urban décor. Glass and chrome light fixtures cast a gentle light between mirrors in black frames. The bar top is covered with polished copper.

The home-grown chef is a Portsmouth native, who designed a menu with "modern cuisine, simply prepared and stylishly presented." He's crafted fine food from Aspen to Paris and now showcases Virginia-made artisan wines, cheeses, and micro beers.

Fresh local ingredients reflect the best of the season's harvest. Seafood showstoppers include a quarter-pound jumbo lump crab cake with sweet corn and country ham, and Chesapeake Bay flounder served with brown butter, hazelnuts, and savory lemon marmalade. Five-spice duck breast is an adventurous marriage of flavors, and the aged beef tenderloin is baptized with a Bowman whiskey peppercorn sauce. Twice drunken bread pudding with rum raisins is the perfect ending to a lovely upscale meal.

Amber Lantern Restaurant

5532 Bainbridge Boulevard
Chesapeake, VA 23320
757-227-3057
www.toprackmarina.com

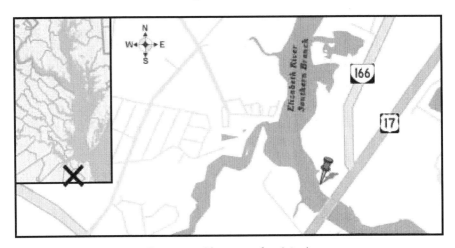

County: Chesapeake (city)
Open: Year Round
Latitude: N 36° 44' 24" ⚓ Longitude: W 76° 17' 45"
Body of Water: Southern Branch of the Elizabeth River
Dockage: Yes
Driving Distance: Richmond: 104 miles,
Norfolk: 9 miles, Washington, DC: 205 miles

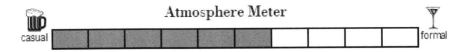

On the second floor above the ship store in a new brown brick building you find the Amber Lantern. It's located next to a massive boatel on the shore of the Elizabeth River. From the outdoor patio, you can watch boats gliding through the water, huge cranes loading barges, and workboats bustling around the marina.

The dining room has a hushed contemporary décor with brown, gray, and gold earth tones. Fiery red light fixtures introduce a splash of color, and the bar is covered with a smooth marble top. Walls are sparsely decorated with small pictures painted in muted hues.

Tapas lead the way to upscale cuisine. Black sesame seed encrusted tuna rests on a delicate bed of seaweed salad, and mussels are sautéed Mediterranean style in a Chardonnay sauce. Lightly fried oysters are served over dill pickle chips. Sweet chili sauce is sprinkled over crispy fried calamari.

Entrees offer a nice balance of seafood and meats. Crab cakes, yellow fin tuna, and Atlantic salmon go head-to-head with juicy pork chops, filet mignon, rack of lamb, and pan-seared duck breast.

Hand-made pasta is this upscale eatery's signature dish. Chunks of Maine lobster are tossed with cheese tortellini, and fruits de mar mixes fresh linguini in a basil pesto sauce with sautéed scallops, oysters, clams, and mussels. Desserts made in-house belong in a culinary hall of fame.

Kelly's Dockside Tavern

136 North Battlefield Boulevard
Chesapeake, VA 23320
757-819-6567
www.kellystavern.com

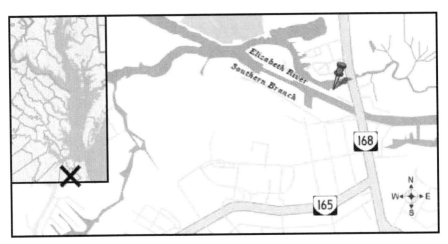

County: Chesapeake (city)
Open: Year Round
Latitude: N 36° 43' 21" ⚓ Longitude: W 76° 14' 31"
Body of Water: Southern Branch of the Elizabeth River
Dockage: Yes
Driving Distance: Richmond: 105 miles,
Norfolk: 10 miles, Washington, DC: 206 miles

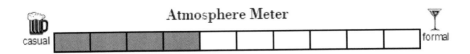

Since it opened in 1983, Kelly's has expanded to
11 locations in Virginia Beach, Norfolk, Chesapeake, Suffolk,
Hampton, and Newport News. That might sound like
a chain, but this eatery sure doesn't feel like one. It's a
charming and inviting place, with a long wooden deck set

right above the water. Tall sweeping trees and townhomes nearby give it a comfortable neighborhood vibe.

The dining area's subtle Irish theme is accentuated by plaid carpet and cushy green leather booths along amber walls. Antique stained glass windows hang from vintage chains and cast a kaleidoscope of color around the room. The artwork is exceptional: vibrant modern bar scenes that make the rooms come alive.

The menu is extensive, offering five pages of selections to meet any diner's taste. Grilled shrimp and salmon with cilantro mango salsa are tucked inside the Fisherman's Wharf Wrap. The Dockside Seafood Platter is loaded with flounder, crab cake, oysters, shrimp, and scallops. Blackened tuna steak has a kick thanks to its tangy wasabi sauce. Half-pound burgers are award-winning, and chicken fajitas sizzle all the way to your table. Key lime pie is tart and refreshing.

In addition to a lovely location and good food, Kelly's has a heart. Its charitable donations help a wide range of community causes, youth groups, animal adoption agencies, local food banks, and the arts.

Big Woody's Bar & Grill

123 North Battlefield Boulevard
Chesapeake, VA 23320
757-436-1919
www.bigwoodys.net

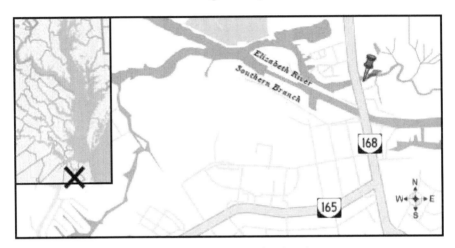

County: Chesapeake (city)
Open: Year Round
Latitude: N 36° 43' 24" ⚓ Longitude: W 76° 14' 24"
Body of Water: Southern Branch of the Elizabeth River
Dockage: No
Driving Distance: Richmond: 105 miles,
Norfolk: 10 miles, Washington, DC: 206 miles

Atmosphere Meter

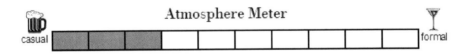

There's so much happening at Big Woody's Bar that it's hard to choose which day to come for a visit. They've got live bands on weekends, beer pong tournaments, DJ dance parties, Tex-Mex Tuesdays, Karaoke Wednesdays, and ladies night on Thursdays From the long wooden deck you can watch boats navigate water locks where the southern branch of the Elizabeth River meets the Albemarle & Chesapeake Canal.

Next door is the Great Bridge Battlefield & Waterways Park. Annual re-enactment events show how American soldiers defeated Lord Dunsmore's band of redcoats in the first Revolutionary War battle fought on Virginia soil. The park also has a boat ramp, picnic area, playground, and trails.

If all these activities leave you thirsty and hungry, you've come to the right place. Hot chicken wings are Big Woody's claim to fame, with flavors ranging from Old Bay to Jack Daniels and Spicy Garlic Parmesan. Big-Bang Shrimp are coated in a spicy-sweet chili sauce, and crab balls are tender and delicious. Crazy Big fish sandwiches are too large to fit inside the bun. Grilled rib yes, burgers, and Philly cheese steaks provide good options for meat eaters.

If you like what you see here, check out Big Woody's new location in the Chesapeake Square Shopping Center.

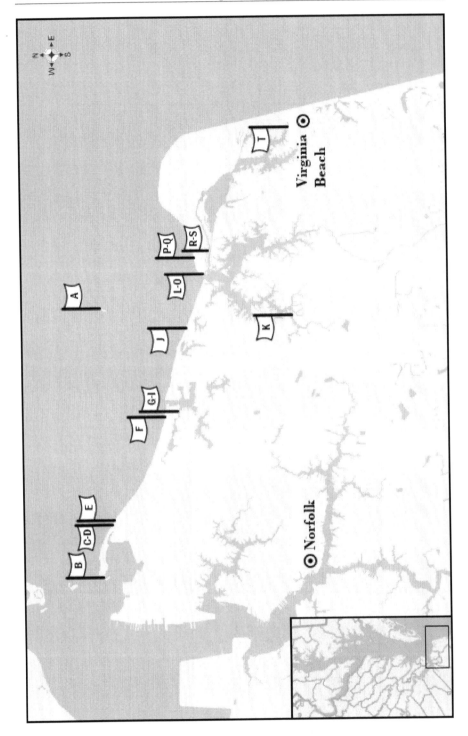

Southside of Hampton Roads

Chesapeake Grill

One Island on the Bay
Virginia Beach, VA 23451
757-318-4818
www.cbbt.com/tour.html

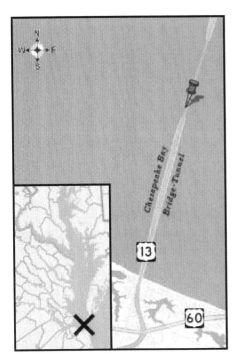

County: Virginia Beach (city)

Open: Year Round

Latitude: N 36° 57' 57"

Longitude: W 76° 6' 46"

Body of Water: directly on the
  Chesapeake Bay

Dockage: No

Driving Distance:
  Richmond: 101 miles
  Norfolk: 16 miles
  Washington, DC: 202 miles

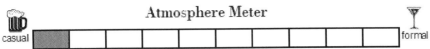

Atmosphere Meter

casual | | | | | | | | | | formal

In 1964, ferry service connecting Virginia Beach to the Eastern Shore stopped running to make way for an amazing new transportation plan. Instead of crossing the waves by boat, travelers could drive their cars on the Chesapeake Bay Bridge-Tunnel. It was heralded as one of the Seven Engineering Wonders of the Modern World because of all the different structures used in one crossing. For about 18 miles at the mouth of the Bay, cars pass through bridges, trestles, tunnels, roads, causeways, and man-made islands.

On the southernmost island about 3.5 miles from Virginia Beach is Chesapeake Grill, located on a magnificent spot with an unparalleled view of the water. You can watch fishermen test their luck on a long cement pier or comb through the gift shop for souvenirs. The restaurant was built in 2010 inside a newly renovated facility for motorists who want to get out and stretch their legs.

The no-frills atmosphere and quick service makes this place a perfect pit stop. You can grab some take-out or enjoy a meal in this unique setting. The menu focuses on Virginia seafood and locally grown ingredients. Crabs, shrimp, and oysters are major players. Soup and salad fixings come from nearby farms, and sandwiches range from pork BBQ to crab cakes and burgers. The seafood platter offers a hearty portion of the region's bounty. It's anything but fancy, but this place belongs on everyone's bucket list.

Sunset Grill

1525 Bayville Street
Norfolk, VA 23503
757-588-1255

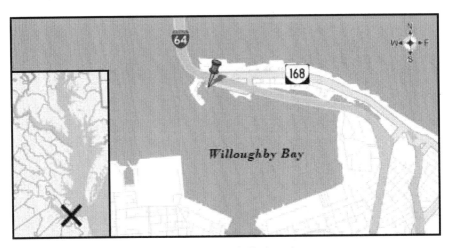

County: Norfolk (city)
Open: Year Round
Latitude: N 36° 57' 56" ⚓ Longitude: W 76° 17' 42"
Body of Water: Willoughby Bay
Dockage: Yes
Driving Distance: Richmond: 82 miles,
Virginia Beach: 26 miles, Washington, DC: 183 miles

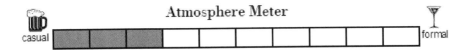

When you see a two-story tan clapboard building in the heart of Willoughby Harbor Marina, then you've arrived safely at Sunset Grill. It's nestled among the sailboat masts and fishing equipment scattered along the water's edge. The restaurant's name is painted on a brightly colored surfboard that hangs above the doorway signaling a touch of Key West on the Chesapeake Bay.

The outdoor deck stretches across the back of the building and faces the water. A recently built wall with windows protects guests from strong winds yet still provides a nice view of the harbor. White twinkle lights are tacked along the top. Tall wooden tables with bar stools offer a good vantage point, and tropical plants underscore the island feel.

The inside dining area is cozy and homey. Its low ceiling is painted sky blue with clouds to give a more open feeling to the space. Eight black leather stools line up along the bar, and cast-iron chairs shaped like scallop shells have seats covered with cheery yellow and white fabric and sailboats. If you hear the cook's got extra jumbo shrimp, don't think about ordering anything else. They're the size of baby lobsters and sweeter than you can imagine. Blackened tuna bites, smoked oysters with brie, and soft-shell sandwiches are full of flavor. Burgers, wraps, and salads are delicious.

Ocean View Fishing Pier Restaurant

414 West Ocean View Avenue
Norfolk, VA 23503
757-583-6000
www.oceanviewfishingpier.com/restaurant.html

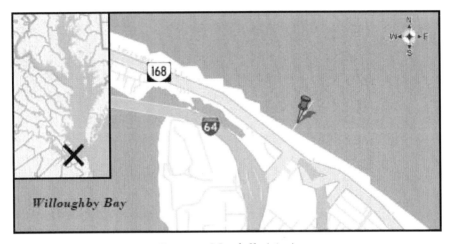

County: Norfolk (city)
Open: Year Round
Latitude: N 36° 57' 42" ⚓ Longitude: W 76° 15' 35"
Body of Water: directly on the Chesapeake Bay
Dockage: No
Driving Distance: Richmond: 84 miles,
Virginia Beach: 23 miles, Washington, DC: 185 miles

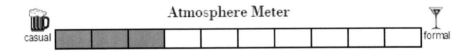

When a serious storm comes barreling up the Bay, we
hold our breath and hope that we don't lose a precious pier,
bridge, lighthouse, or any man-made structure that tries to
defy Mother Nature. In 2003, Isabel's wrath took out Ocean
View Fishing Pier, and Norfolk residents felt like they had lost

a member of their beach family. Fortunately, all 1,690 feet of its wooden planks were rebuilt, and America's longest fishing pier is back in business.

It's a beachside fisherman's paradise in some of the East Coast's most bountiful waters. The bait shop rents all the reels and hooks and stuff you need to catch a big one. If you want to head out to deeper waters, the *Judith Ann* charter boat can take you. But you'll find plenty to do if you stay on the pier. Seven miles of beach, an arcade, and a restaurant with indoor dining and a huge rooftop deck are at your disposal.

This far out on the water, you'll probably have seafood on your mind, but the kitchen does accommodate landlubbers with burgers, steaks, and chicken salad. The rest of the menu features traditional seafood dishes such as sautéed crab cakes, steamed shrimp, grilled tuna, and fried oysters. Everything is well-prepared and has a just-caught freshness. You'll want to leave room for dessert. Eating it slowly buys you time to linger longer at this idyllic location.

The Thirsty Camel Bar & Grill

394 West Ocean View Avenue
Norfolk, VA 23503
757-587-1420
www.thirstycamelnorfolk.com

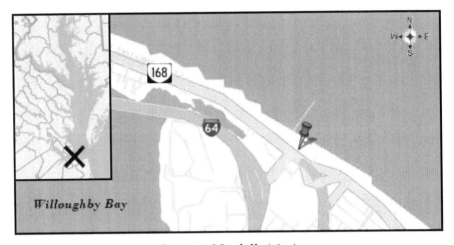

County: Norfolk (city)
Open: Year Round
Latitude: N 36° 57' 35" ⚓ Longitude: W 76° 15' 37"
Body of Water: directly on the Chesapeake Bay
Dockage: No
Driving Distance: Richmond: 84 miles,
Virginia Beach: 23 miles, Washington, DC: 185 miles

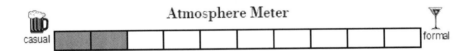

The camel stationed out front doesn't look very thirsty. And the patrons inside seem pretty well hydrated from the bartender's generous pour. The name Thirsty Camel has been painted on the sign since 1960, and everyone seems to like it. The building dates back to 1940 when visitors by the thousands would flock to this area's grand amusement park, beachside boardwalk, and fishing piers. Big bands played in the ballrooms, and sailors on leave from Norfolk Naval Base hoped to steal a kiss from pretty dance partners.

By the 1970s, new highways took tourists farther East to Virginia Beach, the area fell into decline, and the roller coaster was dismantled. Today, the neighborhood's rebirth is well underway with new beach homes and thriving commerce.

The Thirsty Camel survived the changes and remains a local landmark. The building is weathered and worn, but nobody seems to mind. An outdoor deck lets you watch waves roll across the beach and stars appear in the night sky.

Food served at this rustic watering hole is standard pub fare, leaning toward seafood dishes. Humungous steamed shrimp are sprinkled with Old Bay. Soft-shell and crab cake sandwiches are fried golden brown. Wings are seasoned hot or mild, and cheeseburgers come with fries. It's all about cold beer at an oasis of fun on the beach.

Greenies Restaurant & Pub

198 West Ocean View Avenue
Norfolk, VA 23503
757-480-1210

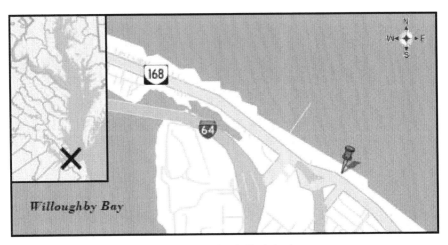

County: Norfolk (city)
Open: Year Round
Latitude: N 36° 57' 23" ⚓ Longitude: W 76° 15' 12"
Body of Water: directly on the Chesapeake Bay
Dockage: No
Driving Distance: Richmond: 85 miles,
Virginia Beach: 22 miles, Washington, DC: 186 miles

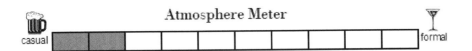

When you get into a beach party mood, head over to Greenies. From the road, the outside of the building might look like an old gas station, but when the band starts pumping tunes and the shooters begin to flow, you'll know you found the right place for an entertaining night out. The crowd is young and energetic, and the upbeat atmosphere is contagious. Five pool tables and a foosball game can keep you busy for hours. Drinks are served icy cold at reasonable prices.

If the noise level inside gets too high or if you just want to cool down, take a seat on the outdoor deck. The Bay breeze is refreshing, and the beachside view is expansive. Statues of a five-piece frog band playing guitars and drums on the roof prove that fun is also encouraged out here. Palm trees planted around the deck's railing set a tropical island tone, and colorful flags flap in the wind above the bar.

The menu keeps things simple with basic bar food and munchies. A pound of peel-and-eat shrimp is seasoned with a heavy dose of Old Bay, and the juicy BBQ pulled pork sandwich requires extra napkins. The Greenie Burger, laden with extra cheese and bacon, is grilled just right. Pizza, nachos, and subs provide ample carbs to burn for a night of revelry and dancing.

The Ship's Cabin Restaurant

4110 East Ocean View Avenue
Norfolk, VA 23518
757-362-0060
www.shipscabinrestaurant.com

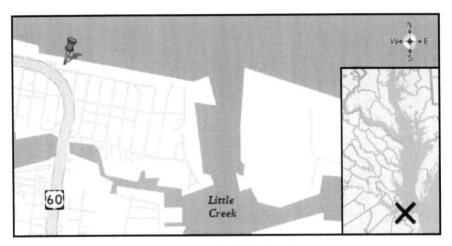

County: Norfolk (city)
Open: Year Round
Latitude: N 36° 55' 52" ⚓ Longitude: W 76° 11' 32"
Body of Water: directly on the Chesapeake Bay
Dockage: No
Driving Distance: Richmond: 88 miles,
Virginia Beach: 20 miles, Washington, DC: 190 miles

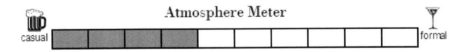

Ship's Cabin's location is hard to beat. You can while away the day at the beach and romp in the Bay's gentle waves. But if the weather doesn't cooperate or you need a break from the sun, you can find plenty of other attractions nearby. Norfolk Botanical Gardens has 155 acres of land and thousands of beautiful plants to see. The 110-year old Virginia Zoo is home to more than 400 animals and receives 500,000 visitors each year. A hidden gem, called the Hermitage Museum, is a 20th century estate with paintings, exhibits, and gorgeous gardens.

After you've worked up an appetite from your excursions, you can grab lunch or dinner at the Ship's Cabin. The building has an old-fashioned quality. A cool blue cruise ship glows from a neon sign, and life rings hang on weather-worn walls outside. The dining room's walls are decorated with nautical artwork and photos of old ships.

The best seats in the house are on the outdoor deck, where yellow and white wooden booths covered with a blue awning face a stunning view of the Chesapeake Bay.

Seafood dominates the menu selections. The cold seafood sampler of oysters, clams, and shrimp cocktail can take the edge off the summer heat. Grilled tuna salad comes with a sesame ginger dressing, and fish tacos are served with rice and beans. If you want to add a little spice to your table, try the Italian specialty dishes. Linguini with clam sauce, shrimp parmesan, and fettuccini alfredo should do the trick. Carnivores can dine on steaks and burgers.

Surf Rider Taylors Landing

8180 Shore Drive
Norfolk, VA 23518
757-480-5000

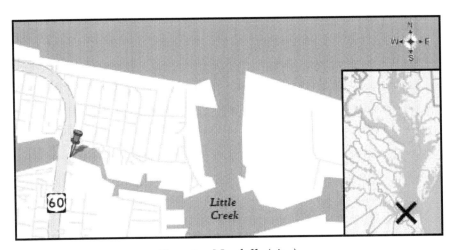

County: Norfolk (city)
Open: Year Round
Latitude: N 36° 55' 28" Longitude: W 76° 11' 28"
Body of Water: Little Creek off the Chesapeake Bay
Dockage: Yes
Driving Distance: Richmond: 89 miles,
Virginia Beach: 19 miles, Washington, DC: 190 miles

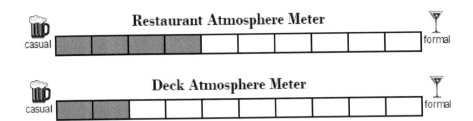

Surf Rider's inside and outside are as different as day and night, so it's up to you to choose which space best suits your mood. The outdoor deck faces a bustling marina, and the atmosphere is charged with energy. A blue and white striped awning casts shade on the tables, and the décor is colorfully creative. The back of the bar stools have palm trees cut into the wood, and a bright blue wall is decorated with hand-painted signs that say "Relax" or "Free Beer Tomorrow." A neon orange couch and rocking chairs in the sitting area create a pleasant place to wait for your table.

The interior dining area has a more hushed ambience and subtle décor. Green leather booths line up along the perimeter of walls painted a soft baby blue. Blond wood tables and chairs fill up the center of the spacious dining room.

The kitchen specializes in seafood, especially crab cakes that are renowned for jumbo lump meat and minimal filler. The Chesapeake Bay Burger is where crabs and cows collide. Cooks kick things up a notch with daily specials such as blackened tilapia with zesty corn salsa, and seafood quiche with shrimp, scallops, and crab. Meatloaf with mac and cheese is packed with flavor, and sweet chicken sandwiches are topped with provolone and bacon. If you like what you find here, Surf Rider has four other locations around the Bay.

Cutty Sark Marina & Grill

4707 Pretty Lake Avenue
Norfolk, VA 23518
757-362-2942

County: Norfolk (city)
Open: Year Round
Latitude: N 36° 55' 27" ⚓ Longitude: W 76° 11' 12"
Body of Water: Little Creek off the Chesapeake Bay
Dockage: Yes
Driving Distance: Richmond: 89 miles,
Virginia Beach: 19 miles, Washington, DC: 190 miles

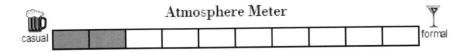

Some people think of Scotch whiskey when they hear the words Cutty Sark. Others envision one of the last great clipper ships built in the mid-1800s to transport tea, wool, and spirits from London to Shanghai before steamships took to the seas. But along Norfolk's waterfront, Cutty Sark is known as a favorite local watering hole.

From the outside it might look like a garden variety marina restaurant with salmon-colored walls and plastic flaps for windows that get unsnapped to let in a breeze. Once you step inside you notice details that make this place unique. A pair of thatched umbrellas stands above the bar. Unfinished pine tables are built around thick wooden pylons. A huge rusty buoy serves as the restaurant's sign. The atmosphere is upbeat and friendly.

Since 1958, the kitchen has cooked fresh seafood bought at the docks from local watermen. The menu is simple, and the dishes are hearty Chesapeake fare.

Crab dip and she-crab soup are nice opening acts to a meal. Sandwich highlights include butterflied shrimp subs, fried oysters, and blackened tuna steak. Mouthwatering burgers and steaks come with fries, and pulled BBQ pork sends you to hog heaven. Hush puppies on the side are crispy treats on your plate. The kids' corner menu offers grilled cheese, chicken tenders, and a classic PB&J.

The Lagoon

9500 30th Bay Street
Norfolk, VA 23518
757-648-8389
www.thelagoon.co

County: Norfolk (city)
Open: Year Round
Latitude: N 36° 55' 26" ⚓ Longitude: W 76° 10' 54"
Body of Water: Little Creek off the Chesapeake Bay
Dockage: Yes
Driving Distance: Richmond: 89 miles,
Virginia Beach: 19 miles, Washington, DC: 190 miles

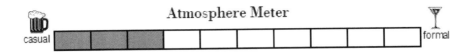

Atmosphere Meter

casual | | | | | | | | | | formal

There's a new kid on the block at Bay Point Marina called The Lagoon, and everyone's invited to stop by. The building used to be home to the Laffin' Gull, but in spring 2012 new owners took the reigns of this lovely waterfront spot.

The atmosphere is casual and family-friendly. In fact, kids get the VIP treatment with a special menu, meals served in a pirate ship, and design-your-own ice cream sundaes with M&Ms, Oreo cookie crumbles, and Gummy Bears. Three cheers to a restaurant that lends a hand with the youngsters!

Patrons young and old like the layout. The spacious main building sports a sky blue roof and floor-to-ceiling windows that create an open airy feel. Views of the sun setting over the marina are exceptional. Extra bonus: a two-tiered tiki deck made of wood and glass that helps set an island tone.

The kitchen pays homage to local seafood delicacies. Appetizers cater to grazers seeking light fare of steamed mussels, mushrooms stuffed with crab, and fried calamari. The cooks pull out all the stops with hearty entrees. Crab cakes, shrimp primavera with linguini, and fried oysters come with coleslaw and fresh-cut fries. Landlubbers can get their fill of burgers and chicken, or sample old-fashioned home cooking in dishes like meatloaf with macaroni and cheese or spaghetti in a red sauce with Italian sausage. Fries smothered with chili and cheese are a diet-busting delight.

Alexander's on the Bay

4536 Ocean View Avenue
Virginia Beach, VA 23455
757-464-4999
www.alexandersonthebayrestaurant.com

County: Virginia Beach (city)
Open: Year Round
Latitude: N 36° 55' 2" ⚓ Longitude: W 76° 7' 35"
Body of Water: directly on the Chesapeake Bay
Dockage: No
Driving Distance: Richmond: 98 miles,
Norfolk: 13 miles, Washington, DC: 199 miles

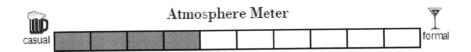

Almost everybody loves a day at the beach, especially with a place like Alexander's dishing up tasty food when you need a break from the sun. Locals like to keep this two-mile stretch of sand secret, because it's not as crowded as others in the region. Chick's Beach was developed in the early 1900s as a waterfront residential community and served as a lookout site during several wars. The only things you need to keep an eye on today are the waves, seagulls, and cars traveling across the Chesapeake Bay Bridge-Tunnel.

Between the restaurant's two indoor dining rooms is an open deck area with tables shaded by umbrellas and a few palm trees. Bands brighten the mood with weekend music. The Bay view at sunset is spectacular. Interior walls are painted in soothing green and beige, with twinkle lights adding a touch of cheer. Tables lit with candles are covered with pastel pink and blue cloths.

The menu is creative and fresh. Home-made paté makes an appearance on the appetizer list, along with local oysters on the half shell, buttery escargot, and jumbo Cajun shrimp swimming in a light cream sauce.

Entrée choices favor just-caught seafood yet offer a few landlubber dishes such as roasted raspberry duckling and filet mignon with sea salt and cracked pepper. Highlights include fresh tuna encrusted with crabmeat and parmesan and Alexander's Amalgamation of shrimp, flounder, crab cake, scallops, and oysters Rockefeller. After you've finished dessert, go ahead and take a final stroll on the beach.

Steinhilber's Restaurant

653 Thalia Road
Virginia Beach, VA 23452
757-340-1156
www.steinys.com

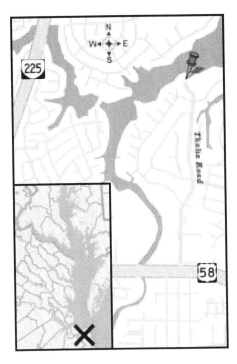

County: Virginia Beach (city)

Open: Year Round

Latitude: N 36° 51' 23"

Longitude: W 76° 7' 13"

Body of Water: Thurston
Branch of the Lynnhaven
River

Dockage: Yes

Driving Distance:
Richmond: 100 miles
Norfolk: 11 miles
Washington, DC: 202 miles

Atmosphere Meter

 casual

 formal

Steinhilber's is the epitome of historic beauty in Virginia Beach. Its doors opened in 1939, making it one of the oldest family-owned restaurants in the state. The founder, Robert Steinhilber, left the city life of Norfolk in 1935 and ventured out to the country, where he bought this property as a weekend retreat for horseback riding, canoeing, and hiking.

Four years later, family chefs started to create recipes for dishes that are presented at your table today.

This place is designed for romantic dinners and intimate conversations. Dim candles and soft twinkle lights set the mood inside, while the patio's plush gardens and starry skies set the stage outdoors for comfortable elegance.

Amorous thoughts might get put on hold when you smell the savory aromas drifting out of the kitchen. The menu reads like a family photo album, with dishes that can spark the appetites of old and new generations. The Original Steiny's Jumbo Fantail Fried Shrimp and its famous sauce has pleased palates for decades, while the étouffée courts more contemporary taste buds with its spicy cauldron of clams, mussels, shrimp, scallops, crawfish, and smoked sausage.

You might have to flip a coin to pick one of three delicious soups: oyster stew, seafood chowder, or she-crab soup. And meat eaters get their choice of beef, bison, or veal. No matter what you order, this is date night at its best, served with grace, charm, and family pride.

Bubba's Seafood Restaurant & Crabhouse

3323 Shore Drive
Virginia Beach, VA 23451
757-481-3513
www.bubbasseafoodrestaurant.com

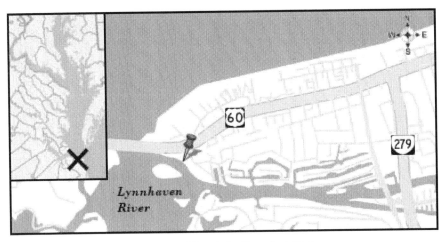

County: Virginia Beach (city)
Open: Year Round
Latitude: N 36° 54' 24" ⚓ Longitude: W 76° 5' 15"
Body of Water: Lynnhaven River
Dockage: Yes
Driving Distance: Richmond: 99 miles,
Norfolk: 14 miles, Washington, DC: 200 miles

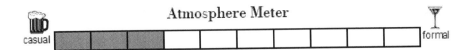

Bubba's neighborhood feels like Seafood Central. Three other restaurants are located on this strip of land along the Lynnhaven River — plus a marina, fishing supply store, and fish markets. Bubba's was one of the first eateries to set anchor here and has become a North Virginia Beach landmark. Its two-tiered waterfront deck and authentic vibe attract locals, tourists, and beachgoers by the droves.

Day or night the view is magnificent. If you want to toast the scenery early in the day, step inside to the Bloody Mary Bar and mix your own eye-opener as hot and spicy as you like. A small bar in the back offers other liquid options. Sunday brunch stars include eggs Benedict, biscuits and gravy, and Bubba's omelet with crab, scallops, and shrimp.

Knotty pine walls covered with fishnets, watermen pictures, and trophy fish add to the laid-back atmosphere. The dinner menu jumpstarts your Bay seafood experience with a raw bar of oysters, clams, and shrimp. You can add a variety of daily catch — tuna, fried oysters, or calamari — to your salad, or pick a dozen steamed crabs in season. The house specialty she-crab soup is heavenly rich.

Meat eaters have a few choices, including grilled chicken breast or the Bubba Burger with cheese, bacon, and crabmeat. But in this seafood-centric domain, your best bet is ordering items caught in local waters.

The Back Deck
Bar & Café

3323 Shore Drive
Virginia Beach, VA 23451
757-481-7512

County: Virginia Beach (city)
Open: Seasonal, March to October
Latitude: N 36° 54' 23" ⚓ Longitude: W 76° 5' 14"
Body of Water: Lynnhaven River
Dockage: Yes
Driving Distance: Richmond: 99 miles,
Norfolk: 14 miles, Washington, DC: 200 miles

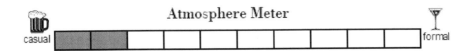

When a restaurant is part of a fish market, you can bet
you're going to get fresh seafood. That's the case with The
Back Deck. It's located behind the Shellfish Company, where

local watermen deliver their daily catch. An open and airy dining room overlooks the water. Walls are painted a cheery yellow, and windows are framed in royal blue. Planters with flowers and ivy hang from wooden beams, and retractable windows open when the weather heats up. It's the kind of place where you're comfortable in flip-flops and shorts.

The kitchen doesn't have a deep fryer, so don't expect to get beer-battered frozen fish. Healthier baked or grilled seafood infused with Tex-Mex flavors is what these cooks prefer. Blackened rockfish and shrimp tacos are washed down with frozen margaritas, and house salad comes with a cilantro lime dressing. Chicken is spruced up with a zesty mango salsa, and paninis are stuffed with tuna salad or Italian deli meats. Tables are covered with piles of discarded shells left behind after eating snow crab legs, steamer clams, and oysters. The feta and shrimp pizza is a big crowd pleaser.

Specialty drinks are regularly tested here. On Mondays you can sample selected wines. Beers such as Purple Haze and Ship Wreck are often on tap. And fruity rum drinks are always on hand for thirsty summer revelers.

Dockside Restaurant

3311 Shore Drive
Virginia Beach, VA 23451
757-481-4545
www.docksideva.com

County: Virginia Beach (city)
Open: Year Round
Latitude: N 36° 54' 21" ⚓ Longitude: W 76° 5' 11"
Body of Water: Lynnhaven River
Dockage: Yes
Driving Distance: Richmond: 99 miles,
Norfolk: 14 miles, Washington, DC: 200 miles

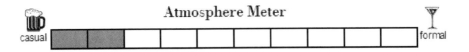

With the letter "D" shaped like a fishhook tempting
a striped bass to take a bite, Dockside's logo sends a clear
message that its top priority is fun on the water. This is the
place to go for nautical adventures. You can spend half a day
on a charter boat fishing for flounder, rockfish, blues, or

whatever local delicacy swims your way. Some of the East Coast's best fishing takes place in these waters. If you'd rather watch than catch, then take a sunset cruise to see dolphins playing in their natural habitat.

Staying on shore offers different, yet quite enjoyable entertainment. You can visit the seafood market and well-stocked wine shop to fill a basket for lunch on the beach. Or you can relax on the waterfront deck with a cold one in hand and listen to live music on weekends. Inside the restaurant you can check out the collection of mounted trophy fish and model sailboats lined up along wood paneled walls.

Having lunch or dinner is also an excellent choice, especially if you're in the mood for just-caught seafood. The Seafood Platter lets you sample a medley of favorites: crab cakes, shrimp, scallops, and the daily catch. Oysters are lightly fried. Tasty imports, like Maine lobster and Alaskan king crab legs, come with an irresistible side of warm drawn butter.

The kid's menu covers the bases with chicken tenders, burgers, pasta, and fried fish. Meat eaters won't leave disappointed after they sink their fork into a juicy New York strip steak, grilled chicken breast, or pasta in a creamy alfredo sauce. Budget-conscious diners can catch an excellent deal if they arrive by 5:30pm and order a discounted Sunset Special.

Chick's Oyster Bar

2143 Vista Circle
Virginia Beach, VA 23451
757-481-5757
www.chicksoysterbar.com

County: Virginia Beach (city)
Open: Year Round
Latitude: N 36° 54' 18" ⚓ Longitude: W 76° 5' 7"
Body of Water: Lynnhaven River
Dockage: Yes
Driving Distance: Richmond: 99 miles,
Norfolk: 14 miles, Washington, DC: 200 miles

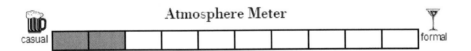

Chick's is a sprawling place, boisterous and fun, with one room flowing into the next. You can sit at a cherry-red leather booth where a menagerie of colorful nautical items, trophy fish, surfboards, and crabs are tacked on the walls. Or join the merriment on the wooden decks above the water and watch boats bustle in and out of the marina. If you're feeling tropical, head back to the tiki bar. No matter where you land, the upbeat vibe will whisk your cares away.

Chick's menu offers local seafood at its best, especially the combo of steamed oysters, clams, shrimp, and mussels. BBQ chicken wraps and Tex-Mex tuna tacos add southwest spice to the mix. Jumbo lump crab cakes and pistachio-crusted mahi mahi are scrumptious. Hand-cut New York strip steaks are flame-grilled with garlic butter, and big bowls of pasta are large enough for two. And try to leave room for the house specialty bread pudding drizzled with whiskey sauce.

It's fitting that a black-and-white, skull and crossbones flag hangs from the rafters of the tiki bar. Lynnhaven's hidden inlets and coves were ideal hiding spots for pirates, and the close proximity to the Atlantic gave 17th century buccaneers easy escape from Chesapeake authorities. Blackbeard was infamous for looting ships and plundering towns along the shores. And not far from this tiki bar, the nefarious French pirate Lewis Guittar was captured in 1699 after a fierce maritime battle with Governor Nicholson.

The Lynnhaven Fish House Restaurant & Pier Café

2350 Starfish Road
Virginia Beach, VA 23451
757-481-0003
www.lynnhavenfishhouse.net

County: Virginia Beach (city)
Open: Main dining area is year-round; pier is seasonal
Latitude: N 36° 54' 47" ⚓ Longitude: W 76° 4' 39"
Body of Water: directly on the Chesapeake Bay
Dockage: No
Driving Distance: Richmond: 100 miles,
Norfolk: 15 miles, Washington, DC: 201 miles

Restaurant Atmosphere Meter

casual | formal

Café Atmosphere Meter

casual | formal

At Lynnhaven Fish House, you can choose between two types of seaside dining and you won't leave disappointed by either experience. The main restaurant area opens with a colorful bang, thanks to a huge stained-glass compass on the ceiling over the bar. Red cushioned chairs with matching red cloth napkins and walls of windows set the tone for casual elegance in a spacious room.

Since 1978, the Kyrus family has specialized in fresh local seafood. You can choose from ten home-made toppings on your fish, from marinara to mango salsa or champagne lobster cream sauce. Award-winning jumbo crab cakes are made with secret seasonings, and hand-breaded fried oysters are plump and delicious. Steaks, pork chops, and chicken are fire-grilled. Signature salads combine crab and shrimp with garden-fresh greens.

A massive channel marker mounted on the roof suggests that Pier Café is a more laid-back alternative. You walk past a fishing pier and small arcade near the entrance and find yourself about 20 feet above the sand on a wooden pier covered by a blue awning. The surround-sound noise of seagulls and waves enhance the long beachfront view. Out here, icy drinks are served in plastic go-cups, and fried fish and chips come in newspaper-lined baskets.

Trade Winds Restaurant

2800 Shore Drive
Virginia Beach, VA 23451
757-481-9000
www.tradewindsrestaurant.com

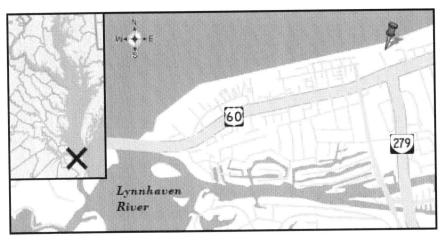

County: Virginia Beach (city)
Open: Year Round
Latitude: N 36° 54' 50" Longitude: W 76° 4' 6"
Body of Water: directly on the Chesapeake Bay
Dockage: No
Driving Distance: Richmond: 100 miles,
Norfolk: 16 miles, Washington, DC: 202 miles

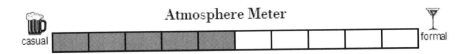

Atmosphere Meter

casual ▮▮▮▮▮▮▮▮ formal

Trade Winds' location is all about beach therapy. You can spend a day lounging in the sun and sand, or you can visit First Landing State Park nearby and enjoy its fishing, swimming, and hiking areas. It's the place where the Virginia Company colonists stepped onto North American soil before settling down in Jamestown, and the scenery remains as beautiful today as it was back in 1607.

The restaurant is located in the Virginia Beach Resort Hotel, which has a modern minimalist feel and a spacious dining area with plenty of room for large parties.

Breakfast, lunch, and dinner are served daily, and Sunday brunch is legendary for overflowing plates of steamed shrimp, smoked salmon, and oysters on the half shell. A chocolate fountain bubbles on a side table, and an omelet chef prepares eggs any way you like. The waffle station with strawberries and blueberries makes kids gasp with joy.

Casual fare centers on seafood but also includes dishes from the land. Grilled fish tacos and crab cake sandwiches are lunch specialties, along with chicken Waldorf salad and portabella mushrooms stuffed with spinach and cheese. Local fish, crabs, and shrimp dominate the dinner menu, and steaks are grilled to perfection. After you finish dessert, head out to the deck to catch a magnificent sunset over the Bay or take a night stroll on the beach.

One Fish-Two Fish

2109 West Great Neck Road
Virginia Beach, VA 23451
757-496-4350
www.onefish-twofish.com

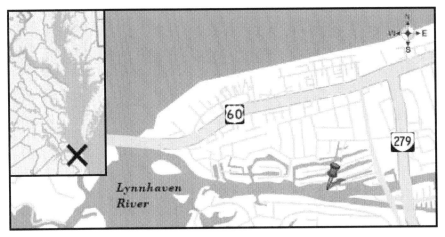

County: Virginia Beach (city)
Open: Year Round
Latitude: N 36° 54' 14" ⚓ Longitude: W 76° 4' 26"
Body of Water: Long Creek off Lynnhaven River
Dockage: Yes
Driving Distance: Richmond: 101 miles,
Norfolk: 16 miles, Washington, DC: 202 miles

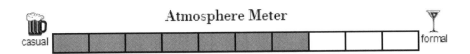

Don't let the name fool you. One Fish-Two Fish might
play tribute to the Dr. Seuss children's classic, but the moment
you step into this sophisticated restaurant you realize that this
place is meant for grown-up taste buds. Since 2000, the chefs
have offered contemporary cuisine with California-inspired

style. The atmosphere is "upscale but not uppity," and the boutique wine list wins accolades for excellence.

The bar's urban feel comes from décor featuring chrome, marble countertops, black metal bar stools, smoky blue glass light fixtures, and modern French paintings on the walls. The dining room's high ceiling and glass walls create an open, airy atmosphere.

From the outdoor deck, you can relax on white Adirondack chairs and catch the panoramic view of a busy marina. Inside you can watch the cooks spin their magic at an exhibition kitchen, which takes center stage in the dining room.

Right before your eyes, the staff whips up light appetizers using local shrimp, scallops, Prince Edward Island mussels, and Virginia oysters. Salads tossed with locally grown vegetables are crisp and fresh. Seafood entree highlights include sautéed shrimp and jumbo lump crab scampi with spinach tagliatelle, and grilled salmon comes with roasted garlic polenta. Beef tenderloin is stuffed with brie, and veal chops come with artichokes.

Finish your meal with sweet treats such as the flourless chocolate torte, vanilla crème brûlée, and strawberry banana cheesecake. Or try a liquid dessert such as the French Kiss (Amaretto, Crème de Cacao, and Baileys) or Express-O Love (Stoli vanilla vodka, espresso, and Frangelico).

Surf Rider Grill,
Marina Shores

2100 Marina Shores Drive
Virginia Beach, VA 23451
757-481-5646

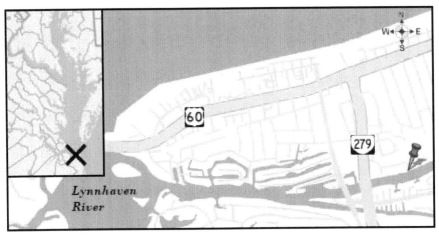

County: Virginia Beach (city)
Open: Seasonal
Latitude: N 36° 54' 21" ⚓ Longitude: W 76° 3' 49"
Body of Water: Long Creek off the Lynnhaven River
Dockage: Yes
Driving Distance: Richmond: 101 miles,
Norfolk: 16 miles, Washington, DC: 202 miles

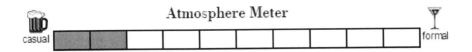

Atmosphere Meter

casual | | | | | | | | | | | formal

This Surf Rider is one of Virginia Beach's best-kept secrets.
It's more casual than the company's other four restaurants,
and locals like it that way. It's a fun place to escape long waits

---

for tables and crowds of tourists. With a signature Rum Runner in hand, you can get your island groove going and watch the boats shuffle in and out of the marina.

The unique, six-sided building is home to a circular bar painted gray with turquoise trim. Rows of booths with matching colors line up around the walls. Dozens of ceiling fans keep the air moving if the plastic window flaps don't let in a strong enough breeze. The mixture of music and laughter creates a lively atmosphere.

Traditional Chesapeake Bay seafood rules the roost here. Fried flounder and grilled tuna steak sandwiches compete for your attention with no-filler crab cakes sautéed to a golden brown. Shrimp salad is cool and refreshing, and fried calamari sports the perfect crunch. Hush puppies are a crispy side for grilled burgers, steaks, and pork chops.

Daily specials add pleasant diversity to the dining options. Don't hesitate to order the salmon with marinara artichoke linguini if you see it on the specials board. And a bowl of creamy she-crab soup is the perfect table partner for fried soft-shell crabs in the spring.

Lighthouse on the Cove

800 Laskin Road
Virginia Beach, VA 23451
757-428-1967
www.lighthouseonthecove.com

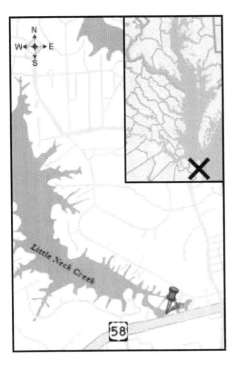

County: Virginia Beach (city)

Open: Year Round; Wed.
  Thurs. and Fri. for dinner

Latitude: N 36° 51' 29"

Longitude: W 75° 59' 13"

Body of Water: Little Neck
  Creek off Linkhorn Bay off
  Broad Bay off the Lynnhaven
  River

Dockage: Yes

Driving Distance:
  Richmond: 107 miles
  Norfolk: 18 miles
  Washington, DC: 208 miles

Atmosphere Meter

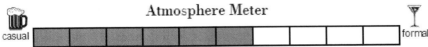

casual   formal

The Lighthouse is a dual-purpose spot. It serves fine food three nights a week and provides a gorgeous venue for special events. What a place for a memorable shindig! It's located on a serene bay inlet lined with sea grass and trees. Oversized windows and a wrap-around deck give a panoramic view of the water. The tall cathedral ceiling and indirect lighting create a magical ambience.

The octagonal-shaped building looks like a screwpile lighthouse and harkens back to a time when these safety beacons aided ships around the Bay. Between 1850 and 1900, 42 lighthouses were built on the Chesapeake's shores (more than anywhere else in the world). The screwpile style was designed to stand steady in the Bay's deep oyster shoals or muddy riverbeds, and the keepers used to live inside year-round with their families. These buildings played an integral role in the region's maritime history.

This lighthouse's menu is more diverse than most seafood houses. Shrimp is cooked three ways: BBQ, Thai, and Buffalo, and tuna bites have a delicate crunch. Salads are garden fresh. Burgers are made from lean ground beef, and golden crab cakes are shy on filling. Cajun salmon is spiced just right, and the 16-ounce Texas rib chop might make you loosen your belt a notch after dinner. Desserts are sweet delights.

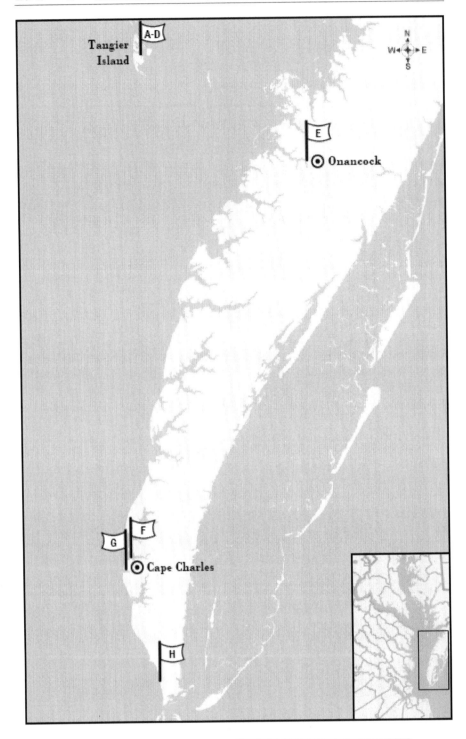

Eastern Shore

Waterfront Restaurant

16125 Main Ridge Road
Tangier, VA 23440
757-891-2248
www.tangierisland-va.com/waterfront

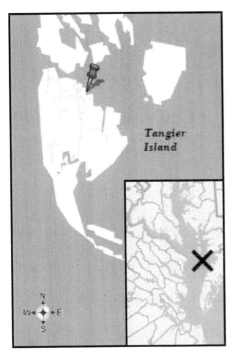

County: Accomack County

Open: Seasonal

Latitude: N 37° 49' 42"

Longitude: W 75° 59' 28"

Body of Water: Tangier Sound

Dockage: Yes

Driving Distance to Reedville
  ferry:
    Richmond: 84 miles
    Norfolk: 97 miles
    Washington, DC: 119 miles

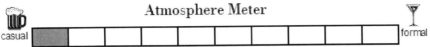

Atmosphere Meter

casual   formal

You can't drive to Tangier Island. Boats, ferries, and planes are the only way to visit this isolated jewel of the Chesapeake Bay. Right next to the ferry dock is Waterfront Restaurant. It's a tiny white building with a deck hovering just above the waves. The view of the quaint village along the shore makes you feel like you've stepped back in time.

You can buy lunch or an afternoon snack here, but you can't purchase a cool beer or any alcohol, because the entire island has been dry for decades. As a trade-off, you can get some of the finest seafood on the planet.

Soft-shell and crab cake sandwiches are the island's claim to fame, because they go immediately from the water to the table. Waterfront's fried shrimp, fish fillet, and clam strip baskets are also tasty bites. Burgers, hot dogs, and chicken salad subs offer options to meat lovers at this casual eatery.

Near the restaurant is a small museum that explains local history. Captain John Smith was the first European to explore Tangier Island in 1608, and named it Russell Isles after a doctor on board his ship. Residents still talk in a dialect of the English language that is similar to what their ancestors spoke in the 1600s. During the War of 1812, British troops occupied the island and launched a successful raid on Washington, DC, and a failed assault on Baltimore from their encampment.

The current population is 727 people, and most of them are crabbers and fishermen who live among the gorgeous marshlands and beaches. The laid-back lifestyle and beautiful scenery make this place a must-see for all Bay explorers.

The Fisherman's Corner
Seafood Restaurant

4419 Long Bridge Road
Tangier, VA 23440
757-891-2900
www.fishermanscornerrestaurant.com

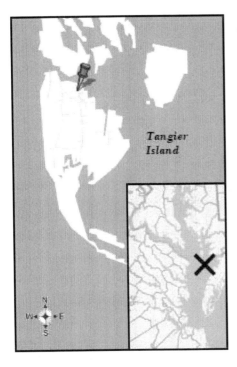

County: Accomack County

Open: Year Round

Latitude: N 37° 49' 43"

Longitude: W 75° 59' 33"

Body of Water: Tangier Sound

Dockage: Yes

Driving Distance to Reedville
ferry:
   Richmond: 84 miles
   Norfolk: 97 miles
   Washington, DC: 119 miles

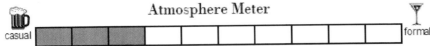

Atmosphere Meter

casual   formal

Guests at Fisherman's Corner can count on down-home cooking made Tangier Island style. The restaurant's allure is a cozy, casual feel with smooth pine floors, rich red walls, and lace curtains hanging on the windows. It's larger than most eateries on the island, with plenty of space for special events and large gatherings.

Kitchen recipes are so delicious that they were recently featured in *Southern Living Magazine,* but the ladies wearing aprons offer one warning: The dish is only as good as the quality of the seafood, so only use genuine Chesapeake catch.

Local crabmeat rules the roost on the menu. You find it blended into a creamy crab dip, padded into crab cakes, or mixed with bread crumbs on top of jumbo shrimp. Soft-shell sandwiches are sensational. Landlubbers can indulge in tender filet mignon, grilled mango-pineapple chicken, and hamburger steak smothered with onions and gravy.

If just eating seafood isn't enough, you can experience a waterman's life for a spell. Ask the restaurant staff about tours where you go out on a working boat to inspect crab pots or examine soft-shells in shedding tanks at a crab shack. The tours offer a unique experience of getting up-close and personal with fishermen who make a living from the sea.

Four Brothers Crab House

16128 Main Ridge Road
Tangier, VA 23440
757-891-2999
www.fourbrotherscrabhouse.com

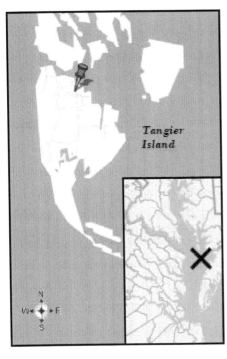

County: Accomack County

Open: Seasonal

Latitude: N 37° 49' 40"

Longitude: W 75° 59' 32"

Body of Water: Tangier Sound

Dockage: Yes

Driving Distance to Reedville
ferry:
Richmond: 84 miles
Norfolk: 97 miles
Washington, DC: 119 miles

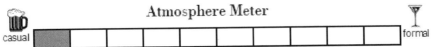

Atmosphere Meter

casual | formal

Four Brothers is more than just a quaint crab house and ice cream parlor. It's the go-to place for all your transportation needs when visiting Tangier Island.

Nobody drives cars here, because the roads and bridges are far too narrow to navigate in an automobile. Instead, golf carts and bicycles fit just right for cruising around the island.

Four Brothers can hook you up with your choice of vehicle. If you want to lounge on the beach, the staff has all the gear you need. Fishing and crabbing equipment are also on hand for guests who want to feel like a waterman for a day.

After you explore the island and work up an appetite, you can grab a bite to eat on the picnic pavilion or wooden deck. It's a lovely place to rub elbows with the locals.

The menu is simple, but it hits the spot. Oysters from the world's finest shoals are served on the half shell. Just a dab of cocktail sauce and a pinch of lemon is all you need to enhance their briny flavor. Crab cakes are simply divine, made of jumbo chunks and a dash of Old Bay. Steamed clams and shrimp come complete with a little melted butter. Burgers, pizza, and BBQ pork round out the casual fare.

The fun begins after you finish the savory portion of your meal. More than 60 flavors of soft-serve ice cream topped with sprinkles await your sweet tooth. Or you can chill out by ordering a thick milk shake or iceberg slush snowball.

Hilda Crockett's
Chesapeake House

16243 Main Street
Tangier, VA 23440
757-891-2331
www.chesapeakehousetangier.com

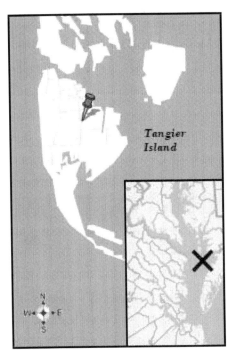

County: Accomack County

Open: Seasonal

Latitude: N 37° 49' 30"

Longitude: W 75° 59' 30"

Body of Water: Tangier Sound

Dockage: Yes

Driving Distance to Reedville
ferry:
   Richmond: 84 miles
   Norfolk: 97 miles
   Washington, DC: 119 miles

Atmosphere Meter

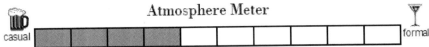

casual   formal

    In New York you've got Rockefeller, and Pittsburgh has Carnegie, but Tangier Island has a cluster of first families who left deep footprints on the region's history. Names like Crockett, Pruitt, Parks, and Thomas pop up everywhere.

Hilda Crockett's eatery bears the name of one of the area's noteworthy residents. John Crockett, the first family member on record to live on the island, bought 475 acres of land in 1778. His descendents farmed the fields and fished the waters, and in 1939 they set up a boarding house that today serves as a restaurant and B&B.

This charming Victorian house with white walls, emerald green shutters, and an old-fashioned screened porch is open to the public seven days a week. The ladies prepare an all-you-can-eat breakfast of scrambled eggs, bacon, potatoes, and crispy fried bread.

Family-style pass-around dinners showcase plates of Chesapeake crab cakes, clam fritters, and Virginia ham, along with home-style sides such as pickled beets, applesauce, hot corn pudding, and butter pound cakes. If you don't want to head home on the afternoon ferry, you can spend the night tucked under the quilt at this historic B&B.

Mallards at the Wharf

2 Market Street
Onancock, VA 23417
757-787-8558
www.mallardsllc.com

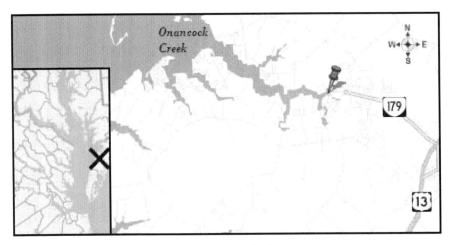

County: Accomack County
Open: Year Round
Latitude: N 37° 42' 43" ⚓ Longitude: W 75° 45' 19"
Body of Water: Onancock Creek off the Chesapeake Bay
Dockage: Yes
Driving Distance: Richmond: 162 miles,
Norfolk: 77 miles, Washington, DC: 184 miles

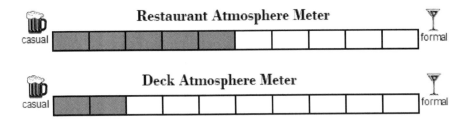

Mallard's building dates back to 1842 when it served as a mercantile store, bank, and meeting place. Today half of the ground floor is home to the Onancock Historic District Welcome Center. Old wooden shelves are filled with antique signs and household items that hearken back to the mid-19th century when Victorian gingerbread homes were built for sea captains and steamboats carried people around the Bay.

Both the upstairs and downstairs dining rooms burst with color. Burnt orange and royal blue walls accentuate the graceful lines that make this old building special. Outside on the waterfront deck, long tan swags of fabric protect the green patio furniture and bar area from the sun's summer rays.

Johnny Mo, a guitar-playing chef, runs the kitchen with a menu that sings of creativity and freshness. Filler-free crab cakes, rockfish tacos, and salmon BLTs are lunch headliners. Roast duck with bourbon glaze is moist and delicious, and four-cheese tortellini is tossed with a harmonious mix of basil pesto cream and toasted walnuts. Grilled swordfish is finished with a dose of cilantro-lime butter.

Take time to stroll around this quaint town that was founded in 1680. Visitors fall in love with its historic homes, churches, cemeteries, and shops. Or head to the wharf and ride a ferry to the beautiful and remote Tangier Island.

Aqua Restaurant & Cabana Bar

900 Marina Village Circle
Cape Charles, VA 23310
757-331-8660
www.baycreekresort.com/dining/aqua.asp

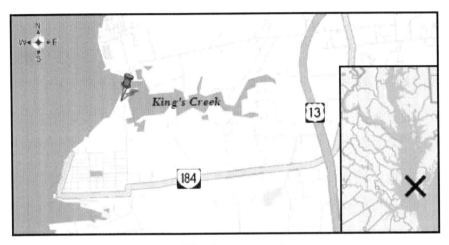

County: Northampton County
Open: Year Round
Latitude: N 37° 16' 45"   Longitude: W 76° 0' 45"
Body of Water: Kings Creek off the Chesapeake Bay
Dockage: Yes
Driving Distance: Richmond: 129 miles,
Norfolk: 44 miles, Washington, DC: 218 miles

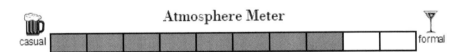

Atmosphere Meter

casual / formal

Aqua is surrounded by luxury homes and manicured lawns, but you get a sense that its designers are more enamored with the sea than the land. Every detail in this gorgeous restaurant feels like a tribute to the beauty of the Bay. Its wrap-around deck faces the water, with white wooden furniture shaded by blue umbrellas that mimic the color of the waves. Guests are treated to a spectacular view of a long sandy beach with breakers made of massive stone piles.

The interior décor echoes the flirtation with Neptune's kingdom. Sea foam colored tiles cover a large pair of pillars and the bar area walls. Modern fish sculptures garnish a cozy sitting space furnished with overstuffed leather chairs. Salt shakers made of cobalt blue glass rest patiently on tables covered with white linen. It's all about comfortable elegance, Chesapeake style.

Lunch and dinner are served daily in this lovely setting, and the chefs know what seafood fans are looking for when choosing dishes made from the watermen's bounty. Local steamed oysters and seaside clams come with drawn butter or cocktail sauce. Signature crab cakes are plump and juicy, and blackened mahi mahi is escorted to the table by pineapple mango salsa and Cuban beans with rice. Bay Creek Bouillabaisse fills a pot with shrimp, mussels, and clams, and simmers them in a white wine tomato sauce. Landlubber treats, like slow-roasted meatloaf with mashed potatoes, Southern-fried chicken breasts, and grilled pork tenderloin with red-eye gravy, bring joy with every bite.

The Shanty

33 Marina Road
Cape Charles, VA 23310
757-695-3853
www.shantycc.com

County: Northampton County
Open: Year Round
Latitude: N 37° 16' 2" ⚓ Longitude: W 76° 1' 12"
Body of Water: Cape Charles Harbor off the Chesapeake Bay
Dockage: Yes
Driving Distance: Richmond: 129 miles,
Norfolk: 44 miles, Washington, DC: 218 miles

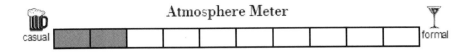

The Shanty says you can "come by boat, car, golf cart, or spaceship." No matter how you get there, it's worth the trip. This laid-back crab house is the new kid on the block in an area that has bragging rights to some of the most gorgeous scenery on the Chesapeake Bay. The waterfront hums with boats, and the town is loaded with colorful turn-of-the-century Victorian homes. The Town Harbor was recently renovated, and a local museum gives the inside scoop about the Bay Coast Railroad's impact on local history.

The red paint was barely dry when The Shanty opened in June 2012. The building is spacious and intentionally rustic. High ceilings are supported by massive wooden beams, and photos of watermen and Eastern Shore life are arranged artfully on blue walls. Kids keep themselves busy with beanbag toss while parents soak up magnificent sunsets.

Food here is simple and easy — pulled straight out of the Bay just before it hits your plate. Oysters on the half shell and fried calamari give you cold and hot options for starters. It's hard to find fresher steamed crabs and shrimp when you're in the mood for picking. Fried fish and chips are nestled into baskets with Caribbean slaw. If you're feeling more like a landlubber than a seafarer, order a plate of spicy chicken tacos, a thick juicy burger, or pulled pork tostadas. With hush puppies on the side, everything is sweeter.

Sunset Grille

32246 Lankford Highway
Cape Charles, VA 23310
757-331-4229
www.sunsetbeachresortva.com/grille

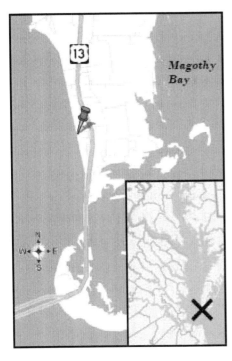

County: Northampton County

Open: Seasonal, Wednesday to
Sunday

Latitude: N 37° 8' 14"

Longitude: W 75° 58' 19"

Body of Water: directly on the
Chesapeake Bay

Dockage: No

Driving Distance:
Richmond: 118 miles
Norfolk: 33 miles
Washington, DC: 219 miles

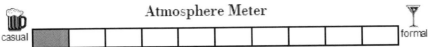

Atmosphere Meter

casual   formal

At the southern tip of the Delmarva Peninsula on
Virginia's Eastern Shore is a little slice of heaven called Sunset
Grill. It's the ultimate get-away, where you leave behind
pressed shirts and panty hose, and get ready to unwind. The
view is glorious: children play on a long stretch of white sand

beach, the Chesapeake Bay Bridge-Tunnel stands off in the distance, and boats tie up near the shore.

Inside the cozy restaurant, sea breezes gently lift fishnets hung above open windows, and locals watch a ball game at the bar. A huge white tent on the deck shields guests from the summer heat. Sunsets are amazing and memorable.

This crab-eater's paradise serves casual Eastern Shore fare with a nouvelle cuisine twist and charges pretty reasonable prices. Just-caught seafood dominates the menu: steamed shrimp, little neck clams, oysters on the half shell, fried calamari, and fist-sized crab cakes. Pulled pork sandwiches, burgers, and hot dogs come with a side of fries. Salad greens are grown in local gardens.

You won't be the first person to get hit with the "I don't want to go home" feeling. A rustic hotel and RV park are conveniently located nearby if you need to extend your visit. Or camp at Kiptopeke State Park, which is a flyway for migratory birds and a fantastic place for hiking and fishing.

Bodies of Water Index

Crab Decks & Tiki Bars of the Chesapeake Bay, Virginia Edition

Cities Index

Restaurant Names Index

<u>Symbols</u>

☣ closed   ☙ private events only

Tiki Tracker

*As you head out on Bay adventures, use this Captain's Log
to keep track of your favorite crab decks and tiki bars.*

Name: _____
Location: _____
Date: _____
Rating: ○ ○ ○ ○ ○
Checklist of things consumed
☐ Steamed Crabs   ☐ Oysters
☐ Crab Cake   ☐ Crab Soup
☐ Beer   ☐ Rum
☐ Other: _____
Comments: _____
_____
_____
_____
_____
_____

Name: _____
Location: _____
Date: _____
Rating: ○ ○ ○ ○ ○
Checklist of things consumed
☐ Steamed Crabs   ☐ Oysters
☐ Crab Cake   ☐ Crab Soup
☐ Beer   ☐ Rum
☐ Other: _____
Comments: _____
_____
_____
_____
_____
_____

Name: _____
Location: _____
Date: _____
Rating: ○ ○ ○ ○ ○
Checklist of things consumed
☐ Steamed Crabs   ☐ Oysters
☐ Crab Cake   ☐ Crab Soup
☐ Beer   ☐ Rum
☐ Other: _____
Comments: _____
_____
_____
_____
_____
_____

Name: _____
Location: _____
Date: _____
Rating: ○ ○ ○ ○ ○
Checklist of things consumed
☐ Steamed Crabs   ☐ Oysters
☐ Crab Cake   ☐ Crab Soup
☐ Beer   ☐ Rum
☐ Other: _____
Comments: _____
_____
_____
_____
_____
_____

Tiki Tracker

Name: _____
Location: _____
Date: _____
Rating: ○ ○ ○ ○ ○
Checklist of things consumed
□ Steamed Crabs □ Oysters
□ Crab Cake □ Crab Soup
□ Beer □ Rum
□ Other: _____
Comments: _____
_____
_____

Name: _____
Location: _____
Date: _____
Rating: ○ ○ ○ ○ ○
Checklist of things consumed
□ Steamed Crabs □ Oysters
□ Crab Cake □ Crab Soup
□ Beer □ Rum
□ Other: _____
Comments: _____
_____
_____

Name: _____
Location: _____
Date: _____
Rating: ○ ○ ○ ○ ○
Checklist of things consumed
□ Steamed Crabs □ Oysters
□ Crab Cake □ Crab Soup
□ Beer □ Rum
□ Other: _____
Comments: _____
_____
_____

Name: _____
Location: _____
Date: _____
Rating: ○ ○ ○ ○ ○
Checklist of things consumed
□ Steamed Crabs □ Oysters
□ Crab Cake □ Crab Soup
□ Beer □ Rum
□ Other: _____
Comments: _____
_____
_____

Name: _____
Location: _____
Date: _____
Rating: ○ ○ ○ ○ ○
Checklist of things consumed
□ Steamed Crabs □ Oysters
□ Crab Cake □ Crab Soup
□ Beer □ Rum
□ Other: _____
Comments: _____
_____
_____

Name: _____
Location: _____
Date: _____
Rating: ○ ○ ○ ○ ○
Checklist of things consumed
□ Steamed Crabs □ Oysters
□ Crab Cake □ Crab Soup
□ Beer □ Rum
□ Other: _____
Comments: _____
_____
_____

Tiki Tracker

Name: _____
Location: _____
Date: _____
Rating: ○ ○ ○ ○ ○
Checklist of things consumed
□ Steamed Crabs   □ Oysters
□ Crab Cake   □ Crab Soup
□ Beer   □ Rum
□ Other: _____
Comments: _____
_____
_____

Name: _____
Location: _____
Date: _____
Rating: ○ ○ ○ ○ ○
Checklist of things consumed
□ Steamed Crabs   □ Oysters
□ Crab Cake   □ Crab Soup
□ Beer   □ Rum
□ Other: _____
Comments: _____
_____
_____

Name: _____
Location: _____
Date: _____
Rating: ○ ○ ○ ○ ○
Checklist of things consumed
□ Steamed Crabs   □ Oysters
□ Crab Cake   □ Crab Soup
□ Beer   □ Rum
□ Other: _____
Comments: _____
_____
_____

Name: _____
Location: _____
Date: _____
Rating: ○ ○ ○ ○ ○
Checklist of things consumed
□ Steamed Crabs   □ Oysters
□ Crab Cake   □ Crab Soup
□ Beer   □ Rum
□ Other: _____
Comments: _____
_____
_____

Name: _____
Location: _____
Date: _____
Rating: ○ ○ ○ ○ ○
Checklist of things consumed
□ Steamed Crabs   □ Oysters
□ Crab Cake   □ Crab Soup
□ Beer   □ Rum
□ Other: _____
Comments: _____
_____
_____

Name: _____
Location: _____
Date: _____
Rating: ○ ○ ○ ○ ○
Checklist of things consumed
□ Steamed Crabs   □ Oysters
□ Crab Cake   □ Crab Soup
□ Beer   □ Rum
□ Other: _____
Comments: _____
_____
_____

Acknowledgements

We'd like to send a heartfelt thanks to all our family and friends for encouraging us to write another book. We extend a bushel of gratitude to Greg and Brenda Hadley for showing us their native Virginian's perspective of the Bay and joining us on many of our research excursions. Thanks to Taylor and Kyle for keeping our boys busy on road trips. Cheers to William and Kay Tyler whose warm hospitality made the last leg of our journey so enjoyable. We're indebted to our dearest friend Rich Barnett, who continues to inspire us and help brainstorm ideas about self-publishing. Samantha Simon gets our appreciation for taking our rough concept and creating the book's fantastic artwork. And a special shout-out goes to Tracy Stannard and Art Cox, who believed in us at the beginning and helped spread the word about crabs and tiki.